*I Told You So*

# I Told You So

## Kate Clinton

Beacon Press · Boston

**Beacon Press**
25 Beacon Street
Boston, Massachusetts 02108-2892
www.beacon.org

**Beacon Press books**
are published under the auspices of
the Unitarian Universalist Association of Congregations.

© **2009 by Kate Clinton**
All rights reserved
Printed in the United States of America

13  12  11  10     8  7  6  5  4  3  2  1

**This book is printed on acid-free paper that meets the uncoated paper**
ANSI/NISO specifications for permanence as revised in 1992.

**Text design by Susan E. Kelly**
of Wilsted & Taylor Publishing Services

**Library of Congress Cataloging-in-Publication Data**
Clinton, Kate.
I told you so / Kate Clinton.
p. cm.
ISBN-13: 978-0-8070-4455-1 (paperback: alk. paper)
1. American wit and humor.  I. Title.
PN6165.C63 2009
814'.6—dc22
2008041102

**For Urvashi Vaid**

*who told me so*

# Contents

## 47 *Bawdy Politics*

## 71 *Sisterhood of the Traveling Pantsuit*

## *169 Come On, Rogue*

# Introduction

*I Told You So* was completed at the end of July 2008. This book is a collection of columns from magazines, essays translated from early-century Bloggerean, and material written especially for this compilation. After I sent the document file of my book to my editor just by warily pressing Send, I made a big flourish of checking off the last day of my six-month writing schedule. I cleaned off my desk, filed two trees' worth of hard-copy rewrites, and turned my full attention to writing for my summer show in Provincetown.

For more than twenty years I have performed in July and August in Provincetown. I write something new every day, especially if the weather is bad; I ride my bike down to the club and try the lines out at night. My audience knows that a lot of the material is being work-shopped for the show I will take on the road in the fall. They know because generally I tell them.

Some weeks a brilliant three pages of newly minted material becomes an aside after only three shows. But other times a throwaway line gets a surprising response and over a few performances grows to a brand-new ten minutes. My audiences like being part of the process. They often talk to me after a show: "When you said that, I thought you were going to go this way," as if the show were on MapQuest, but then they finish with the perfect punch line that had eluded me. Since I have joke dyslexia, they kindly point out when I have reversed setup and punch line altogether. Or they tell me their stories. I take notes. I promise them royalties.

My partner of twenty years has said to me after almost every show she has seen, "Well, that was too long, but you need to do more political stuff." Over the years, and because of the world, I have become more political. Actually I am a full-blown junkie. My shows reflect that. On the Provincetown entertainment menu of drag shows, piano

bars, Broadway adaptations, theater, and comedy, I am the entrée known as "that political one."

In the past, doing a lot of political material for people on their precious one- or two-week vacation in a resort town could be dicey. They have been at the beach all day reading trashy beach books or boogie boarding. They have not kept up. Some nights I felt that I was anchoring a news show, not so much doing a comedy show. Instead of laughter, I would hear, "I wish she had this on PowerPoint."

The summer of 2008 was like nothing I had ever witnessed. It was not just because critical mass had been reached in the possession of personal handheld devices. Nor was it because the town mothers and fathers had finally gotten some decent radio transmitters and fewer people had to stand out in parking lots screaming into their cell phones, "I can't hear you!" That summer Wi-Fi was *the* preferred guesthouse amenity. More than a private bath. No one wanted off the grid. No one wanted to miss anything. Even on vacation.

Would the Hillary supporters get over themselves and make the change to Obama? Could Obama really beat McCain? The town slept fitfully, waiting for a text message about Obama's choice for vice president. Would he pick Hillary? In the line at the Grand Union, strangers would say, "Can't wait to hear what you have to say about Palin." Increasingly panicked mass e-mails from California warned of the passage of Prop Hate, the anti-gay-marriage ballot initiative. Everyone bemoaned high gas prices. Bear Stearns Week trumped the fun of Bear Week. International tourists crowded town during Carnival Week. Some shops accepted euros. In one ominous sign, the store called Don't Panic was shuttered.

When your situation room is a resort town in August, it is difficult to convey the seriousness of some developments to vacationers. It is also perhaps cruel. In one late August show I joked about George W., back stateside from the Chinese Olympics, which had been brought to us by our own credit card debt. With not one little toenail left on his moral footprint, and still president-erect from cruising the Olympic volleyball babes and hectoring China on its human rights abuses, our spectator in chief excoriated Russia for its preemptive strike on Georgia. You could practically hear the world snorting, or maybe it was me.

After the show, I was talking to one very sunburned woman and realized she thought Russia had invaded the state of Georgia. (No, it was not Sarah Palin.) She confided, "If they can fix the Atlanta airport, I'm all for it. They should give them Florida while they're at it." But even at half-attention, people were more politically and passionately interested in politics than I could recall.

After Labor Day and before my tomatoes had ripened, dammit, I finished my summer-long run and returned to Manhattan with a shiny new show for fall touring. But every day brought such dizzying change, I wrote new material and eased out pieces that seemed dated with just a week's shelf life, because the show was getting as long as a Bruce Springsteen show. I felt like an embedded war correspondent just a sentence or two ahead of breaking news.

Whenever I thought back to some sections of the book I had had to turn in at the end of July, they seemed like all setup without punch line, cruel foreplay. I regretted not being able to finish the Clinton-Obama/McCain-Palin/Prop Hate/campaign/election story lines. It seemed unfair, unfinished.

As we who wanted a woman president almost learned from Sarah Palin, be careful what you wish for. In early September, I received a call from my editor at Beacon Press requesting an additional chapter to conclude the political dramas I had been following. Though I had a busy fall tour schedule, it was like receiving a reprieve from the governor. And at sixty, I find I work well on deadlines.

The stay of publication also allowed me to move on. This time, when I finished the last chapter, the book felt finished. I felt finished. Eight long years of being Kate the Designated Bush Watcher can make you very cynical. Yes it can. I am finished living in I-told-you-so. The schaden is off my freude. I am eager to transition into my new job: Kate the Happy Chronicler of the Successes of the Bush Toxic Cleanup Committee, the Great Restoration Hardware Voting Rights Act, the International War Crimes Tribunal, the Truth and Reconciliation Commission, the Actual Intelligent Design Project, the Stepping Aside of the Baby Boomer Ritual, and the Cynicism Abatement Task Force.

*I Told You So*

# *MSM*

The mainstream media is so very busy—inventing, inverting, repeating, polling, split-screening, poking high-tech election night Ouija boards, immoderating debates, self-justifying, fear-mongering, bloviating, memorializing, supersolipsizing, anonymous sourcing, sucking up, swarming, and riding high on a double-decker Straight Talk Express—that it has taken to calling itself, without apparent hint of irony, the MSM. In public-health circles, MSM stands for "men who have sex with men." The Tuckers, Aarons, Andersons blur. Katie hits a flat-panel plasma ceiling. A herd of independent minds, fearful for jobs threatened by new multiformatted information delivery systems, moronically converge and make a horse race out of an election. Who Should Win places second to Who Will Win and is euthanized off-camera. How low can we go? Limbaugh lower now.

# Democracy Diet

## May 2005

In *Fat Actress,* Kirstie Alley lashes out at Hollywood's obsession with thinness. As a self-proclaimed fat actress, she knows whereof she speaks. Her show is a sweet and sometimes sour revenge. She serves it up cold.

Her audience, which is never going to be too rich, seems to be going for the too-thin option, and cannot take its eyes off her and how large she has gotten. Viewers are grimly invested in her weight loss.

Nielsen has not yet released any figures on the gender breakdown of the declining viewership of *Fat Actress,* but I suspect a lot of desperate housewives are tuning in. Kirstie Alley–watching has replaced Oprah-watching, since, to the secret disappointment of many, Oprah's weight seems to have stabilized. Dr. Phil, who coached Oprah in her Texas meat disparagement trial, was rewarded for his success with his own bossy, annoying show, another entrant in the dieting industrial complex. I never thought I would miss Richard Simmons.

The zaftig Ms. Alley's show is the latest subset of the dieting-as-acting school. In the movies, it all started when Robert De Niro gained weight for his role as Jake LaMotta in *Raging Bull.* Tom Hanks lost weight for his Oscar-winning part as a person with AIDS in *Philadelphia* and then as the marooned Federal Express man in *Cast Away.* Charlize Theron gained weight and lost the makeup for her performance as serial killer Aileen Wuornos in *Monster.* The already thin Daniel Day-Lewis is even thinner as Jack in *The Ballad of Jack and Rose.* Renée Zellweger yoyoed up and down for the role of the insipid Bridget Jones. Weight Watchers is the new method acting. Fergie is a fat-free Uta Häagen-Dazs.

A new entrée on the very full menu of weight-loss books, Mireille Guiliano's best-selling *French Women Don't Get Fat,* is *une autre* bee-otch slap in the Franco-American wars. She impugns plus-size American women when she wearily opines that French women "have learned to manage and gratify their senses. They eat with all five of their senses." No mention of the impact that has had on table settings or manners.

On the eve of 2005, George Bush said that his New Year's resolution was—no, not ending the war and bringing the troops home, silly—to lose a few pounds and stay away from sugar! His "No Fat Child Left Behind Federal Nutritional Guidelines," however, are more daunting than helpful—fresh selections from the five vegetable subgroups, a variety of whole grains, and vigorous sixty-minute workouts. I read the guidelines and wanted a big grab bag of Cheetos.

The Bush doctrine of cutting taxes to reduce revenue, with the goal of reducing the size and number of services offered by government, is what is known in the conservative mainstream as "starving the beast." When a beast is starved, it gets cranky and lashes out. Kirstie Alley has. That, more than her weight loss, is what is so fascinating. I am hoping the beast we call democracy snaps back at its tormentors and takes back the zoo.

# I Want My Gay TV

## July 2005

Good news for anyone chanting, "I want my gay TV!" We will soon have not one but three new gay channels!

Despite the public bonhomie among the three ("there's room for everybody, every one will find a niche"), they are all rushing to get on the air first. Initially I worried that the programmers would take any old proven television formula, add a gay, a couple of rainbows, and be good to go—*Gay Friends, The Gay Shandling Show, Really Judging*

*Gay Amy, Gay Ellen.* Those shows were pitched and nixed. A few got through, but the new channels are also developing TV that reflects our lives and tells our stories. And these days, *Gay Survivor* seems so redundant.

Here! TV, established in 2002, is a pay-service cable network. Viewers can subscribe or purchase individual on-demand programs. In addition to its gay and lesbian film library, Here! is developing original programming. Its ambitious goal is six new series and twelve new films per year. Already in the can are shows on gay parenting, a supernatural soap opera, a gothic horror series, a naval action drama, a drama about a rogue asteroid, and a hard-boiled detective series. Here! also plans to film live drama and comedy.

Q Television Network, launched in late 2004, proudly self-identifies as "a gay lifestyle" channel for gays, lesbians, bisexuals, transsexuals, and the curious. It is available on the satellite service RCN in Boston, San Francisco, and New York and is soon to expand to Denver, Washington, D.C., and Seattle. It covers gay travel, gay sporting events (including bowling), and gay pride festivals. In addition, it plans to host live broadcasts, though its morning show's title, *Good Morning Gay America,* was spiked by ABC for copyright infringement. It is now known simply as *Gay Day.*

Unlike the other gay-per-view channels, Logo, from the cable giant Viacom, is an advertiser-supported basic cable channel. It will broadcast its movie library as well as an ongoing documentary series, specials, narrative shows, newscasts, and reality shows. Its February launch date was postponed to late June for programming reasons and because Logo experienced difficulties getting into some markets: aka, "A gay cable channel? Over my dead body." Some reps informed Logo that there were no gays in their markets. I think that was the Cheney Ponderosa in Wyoming.

Of course, everybody does not love our gay monde. Among others, the American Family Association's head PEO (Puritan Executive Officer) Tim Wildmon, who warned that late-night gay channels could turn pornographic, given that "the very nature of homosexuality is based on eroticism and the infatuation with sex." Apparently his cable package does not have HBO's *Sex and the City* or ABC's *Desperate Housewives.*

I hope the new formats will offer an opportunity to showcase some

of the daring LGBT plays and performances that are often seen only live. Think *Playhouse Gay 90s.*

My fear is, in this very extreme time for gays, that TV is too medium. It can suck the life force out of the populace and be a portal to passivity. TiVo is not activism. Virtual community is not real community.

If masses of LGBT protesters appeared every Sunday as the local religious right JumboTrons were cooling down from spewing anti-gay rhetoric, and the security guards were overheard saying to one another, "That cursed religion show on Here! must have just signed off," I might feel better. If statehouses were flooded with gay marriage advocates and judges were heard mumbling, "It's that damnable *Take Back Your Government* show on Q television," I might feel better. Or if women's health centers were suddenly guarded by LGBT health vigilantes and besieged providers were heard saying, "Thank goddess for that Logo *Health Show*—here's a condom," then we would be onto something. Until then, let's enjoy our gay TV but not neglect to continue the activism that has made it possible.

........................................................................................

# We're Back in Kansas, Toto

## September 2005

Lots of my friends have read and loved Thomas Frank's bracing book, *What's the Matter with Kansas?* As is well documented in Frank's book, his native state's rectitudinous rectangularity has morphed from its early radical progressivism to its current radical conservatism. When asked, my friends can restate the premise of the mutation: The right wing expertly manipulated culture issues—gay marriage, evolution, patriotism—to avoid real-life economic security issues. But a nagging "Huh?" bothers me. Like all those postelection Democrats visiting the Lakoff and Wallis shrines, I thought if I could really answer the Kansas conundrum, we might be able to parse the election. And of course people would start paying big bucks to visit my shrine.

I do not count myself one of the root-cause coastal liberal snobs, and maybe that is the way all coastal liberal snobs think. I love performing in Kansas City. It is a town that has enough civic confidence and flexibility to locate itself in two states. I can vouch that New Yorkers would not be so well disposed to an Albany, Massachusetts.

KC used to be the 7-Eleven stop on everyone's westward trek. When the kids in the way back of the Conestogas whined, "Are we there yet?" the family would stop in KC to resupply for the rest of the journey.

The gay population, so besieged in Kansas, is vibrant and feisty. After all, Fred Phelps, his family, and their national Kill Fags Tour hail from the state capital, Topeka. No one knows whose payroll he is on or where he gets his frequent-flier miles. His answer to the question "What's the matter with Kansas?" is, of course, Dorothy.

During a bit of free time before one of my shows, I was roaming around KC, idly wondering why people vote against their own best economic and political interests. That is when I came upon Hallmark headquarters. Founded in 1910, Hallmark has grown to be the dominant force in "the personal expression industry—helping people express their feelings and touching the lives of others." It owns Crown Media of *Hallmark Hall of Fame* fame and Crayola and all its colors, which might explain the garishly forced cheeriness of the town. I think I am onto something. *CSI: Kansas City*!

It is my wildly undocumented hunch that Hallmark factories have been illegally dumping in the Missouri River, contaminating the groundwater and thus infecting the population. If I could afford the forensics experts, I bet they would find foiled hearts, glitter effluvia, doily fragments, and inordinately high levels of schmaltz in the outflow. And if I could hire those dogged, laid-off weapons-of-mass-destruction searchers, I have a hunch they would find a secret cache of highly suspicious cards in a spider hole on the Hallmark grounds.

Here is a selection:

**Pre-birthday cards**

*You never believed that cytoblastphemy*
*When you adopted your egg*
*You just called her Mimi.*

**Home school graduation cards**

*You took the test, you did your best.*
*In all the crowd, you did me proud.*

Also available:

**Embossed home school reunion invitations, come in packs of one or two.**

**Intelligent Design cards**

*Why roses are red,*
*Or the sky is so blue.*
*Don't worry your head*
*When you haven't a clue.*
*I think it's God, don't you?*

My Hallmark intel people tell me that a new Over My Dead Body ("Gays will get married"/"Hillary will be president"/"I'll give up my Uzi") humorous line of cards is in the works. Cards are also planned for On Your Secondary Virginity, Your Covenant Marriage Anniversary, Fatherland Day, Invitation to a Book Burning, and Countdown to the Rapture.

......................................................................................

# The Passion of the Penguins
## October 2005

If my recent movie attendance is any indication of the national box office receipts, Hollywood can put a fork in it. They're done. Since *Wedding Crashers* did not seem to be about gay marriage and *The War of the Worlds* and *The Brothers Grimm* seemed redundant, I only went twice to the tiny Provincetown New Art Cinema all summer.

I did see *The March of the Penguins,* set in the Antarctic, which

seemed like a good antidote to the unrelated-to-global-warming, sticky, freaky, blast furnace of summer we had. But despite all the anthropomorphizing going on around me, I could not identify with this film. With its emphasis on procreation, monogamy, and heart-melting scenes of male penguins caring for their young (for three months of the year), the documentary is relentlessly straight. Perhaps that is why it has become the next big date movie among fundamentalists: *The Passion of the Penguins*.

Then I saw *The Aristocrats*. And that seemed like a good antidote to the serious world intruding on the crazy, hazy, lazy days of summer. But again, I could not identify.

First, *The Aristocrats* is not a movie about the Bushes. It is a documentary about the world's filthiest joke and the comics who love it. A show-biz family goes to a vaudeville talent agency. The agent asks the father to describe their act. The father proceeds: The family dog is trained to poop in their son's mouth while the boy is copulating with their nine-year-old daughter, and all the while the father is urinating on the mother, and on and on. The agent asks the father what they call themselves. The father announces with flourish, "The Aristocrats."

The filmmakers, skeptic Penn Gillette and comic Paul Provenza, became re-intrigued with the joke at a Friar's Club roast of Hugh Hefner three weeks after 9/11. At the roast, Gilbert Gottfried, a squinting tummler with a shrieking ferret shtick, was scorching old Hugh. But the crowd was quiet. He made a joke about bombing, then something about 9/11. There were hisses from the crowd. Someone shouted, "Too soon." Desperate, Gottfried lapsed into the old tried-and-true and began a rendition of the Aristocrats joke. Oh, he saved the day. That Gilbert. In a new world of uncertainty, fear, terror, and attack, the reassuring familiarity of the old joke was a balm to the male spirit.

The joke is as predictable as a comedy threesome, as formulaic as a knock-knock. It has three parts: the setup, the hilarious description of the troupe's act, and the two-word punch line. If the teller observes the rules of setup and punch line, he is allowed between those two levees of levity total comic license to spew a toxic bilge of excrement, sexism, misogyny, bestiality, violence, and pedophilia.

The joke is a secret handshake, an insider joke, #23 in your comedy hymnals, the joke comics tell to amuse each other after hours.

The film is an unwitty, unwitting passport through comic portals into a puerile world. Good little boys like *Full House*'s Bob Saget and *Mad About You*'s Paul Reiser, who found fame in bland sitcoms, get to show that when freed from the terrible style-cramping burden of political correctness, they can be as vile as any of their good-old-boys-club friends.

Critics both of and in the movie claim that the constant repetition of the joke has the effect of taking away the hurtful meaning of the words. That is, saying "banging your nine-year-old daughter" many times eventually erases meaning, so the focus can be on the amazing variety of comic styles. The ultimately practical joke of rape is not the point. Oh, okay.

Because it is a primer of mainstream comics and comedy writers, I went to *The Aristocrats* as part of my ongoing professional research and development. The walls of the New Art Cinema are quite porous, and often when I was supposed to be laughing, all I could hear was booming, rumbling blasts from the theater next door, signaling the end of the world.

............................................................................................................

# Why You'll Never Hear "Heeeeeeere's Katie!"

### February 2006

When I was ten years old, I begged to stay up to watch *The Tonight Show* with Johnny Carson. My father said that I was too young. I reasoned with him that when I was old enough to watch, I would be too tired. My argument won me a one-time-only Friday-night reprieve. I popped up early Saturday morning to show that despite my late night, I could still be a productive member of the household. During the years when I was old enough to watch and young enough to stay awake, I watched for women—Moms Mabley, Phyllis Diller, Anne Meara, Elaine May, Totie Fields. With the aid of VCRs and TiVo,

I have continued my personal longitudinal study of late-night comedy shows. As a feminist who has made her living in comedy for twenty-five years, I wonder, why is it that women comics never get to make that leap to hosting a late-night talk show?

Did the late-show pioneers—Steve Allen, Ernie Kovacs, and Jack Paar—sign a secret pact to keep women off the nocturnal transmissions, thus begetting Joey Bishop, Dick Cavett, and Johnny Carson? Carson crushed his loyal guest host, Joan Rivers, like a bug and sent her off to shill jewelry on QVC and interview others who were famous for being famous on award-show red carpets. Then, after a public cat-fight, he bequeathed his show to Jay Leno, not David Letterman, who got his start doing the weather in Indianapolis, toiling in the morning talk-show fields. Now Leno, in an oddly lame-duck move, has already bequeathed the hallowed slot to the younger, hipper (to some) Conan O'Brien.

Letterman has not yet named his successor but will probably select another stud from the stable, since cable channels, hoping to establish late-show cred, have followed the lead of the big three channels with yet more men: Arsenio Hall, Dennis Miller, Craig Kilborn, Gary Shandling, Jimmy Kimmel, D.L. Hughley, and Jon Stewart. Bill Maher, who lost *Politically Incorrect* after an untimely politically incorrect comment on the courage of high-altitude bombers, is back with another show called *Real Time*. Even if these guys fail, they fail into another show.

Why is that?

Joan Rivers, who followed Johnny's sacrosanct formula of opening monologue and guest interview, was canceled. So when Whoopi Goldberg hosted a short-lived late-night show she tried something new, upending the bandleader-sidekick-desk-panel seating arrangement. Unfortunately, she also experimented with interviewing one guest for a full hour. If viewers did not like her guest, they switched channels. A terrible faux pas, when the whole point of these shows is to advertise stuff to nineteen-to-thirty-four-year-old males, the ones who supposedly watch these shows—although can anything really compete with online porn? Whoopi was not renewed. Paula Poundstone and others have also tried and failed to guess the secret password into the after-hours club, but the bouncers are fierce.

Apparently estrogen does not show well under the night lights

and testosterone withers in the light of day. So women comics are relegated to daytime talk shows. Despite Rosie O'Donnell's and Ellen DeGeneres's big hits, they are not allowed to stay up late with the guys. Is it women's fate to speak only to the daytime audience of the underemployed, freelancers, school truants, and stay-at-home moms? Is it somehow unseemly for women to speak to men at night?

Can the answer be found in *The Aristocrats?* As discussed, by a process of natural selection, the fittest survivors of the film's comic Darwinism, the aristocrati of comedy, are mostly male. The comic elders mouth the classic line, which I have often heard in my career, "Look, funny is funny." That gender erasure reminds me of something June Jordan once said: there is power and there is point of view, and whoever has the power determines the point of view. So the ejaculatory, stand-up/punch-line brand of male humor has a funny point of view. The multiorgasmic, extended storytelling of women does not have a funny point of view. Because the long, multipart, middle section of the aristocrat joke is safely bracketed by the familiar setup and punch line, when men tell it, it is deemed hilarious.

Of the women comics in the film, only Goldberg and Sarah Silverman make the joke their own—Goldberg by anthropomorphizing foreskins and Silverman by inhabiting the role of the aristocrats' waiflike, wounded daughter. The rest of the women try to tell the joke from the male point of view and come across as uncomfortable consorts, afterthoughts.

Call it the Heisenberg Humor Principle: men find men funny because that is what they are looking for. The men who own the networks that produce the late-night TV shows recognize the male point of view, and they promote it to the coveted position behind the desk. With age and an undiminished feminism, I have been able to shift the frame. I now sleep well, knowing that all that tawdry humor is safely consigned to the after hours. Last one in, turn out the lights.

.................................................................................

# Hikikomori

## February 2006

When I was four or five, I was fascinated by sporadic *National Geographic* stories of the lone Japanese soldier emerging from some island jungle to surrender years after the war was over. He squints into the sun, waving a tiny shred of white, frail but proud in the immaculate tatters of his uniform. I was so embarrassed for him. It is painful to be the last to know. I never wondered how the photographer happened to catch that moment.

And—full disclosure—in this era of Oprah-okayed emotionally redemptive "truth," and given my unreliable memory, perhaps it was a scene from the movie *Heaven Knows, Mr. Allison* I rented from Netflix. I do not know.

Recently my youthful iconography has been updated by the new phenomenon of *hikikomori*, a Japanese word meaning "withdrawal." Ironically, the withdrawal syndrome is finally coming out of the closet in Japan. Given the media tendency toward laziness and its attendant swarming, many stories about this phenomenon of withdrawal have appeared recently. No telling if it is as catastrophic as it is portrayed.

It certainly must be for the parents of the (mostly) boys who in their teens retreat to their rooms for years at a time, occasionally venturing out to the convenience store for a to-go bento box if their parents are trying last-ditch tough love and are no longer leaving meals outside their bedroom doors. Experts in the *hikikomori* treatment industrial complex, which has inevitably grown with the disorder, posit that the condition is caused by a perfect storm of Japan's sagging economy, job insecurity, parental and school pressures, declining birthrates, and feelings of humiliation.

Equally fascinating is the role of the "rental sister." After a distraught parent telephones a *hikikomori* help line, these women are dispatched as outreach counselors to the boy's home to try to coax

him out of his self-imposed exile. The rental sisters, who sound like distant cousins of comfort women, have more success than the few rental brothers. They will talk softly and persistently through the boy's bedroom door for weeks and months. Whatever it takes. If the boy emerges, he is then encouraged to attend day-care programs to help him learn real-world coping skills.

Whether it is out of the jungle or out of the bedroom, my interest in the updated surrender-to-the-world motif comes, not from any orientalism, but rather from an abiding interest in postimperialism. I find myself studying postimperial cultures—the Ottoman Empire, Portugal, England, the New York Yankees, the Ford Motor Company—for signs of what a postimperial America will be like in my waning years.

It seemed we were already in our own postimperial hikikomoric moment. In the sagging U.S. economy and uncertain job market, a rash of articles and specials about "the boy crisis" began appearing. Boys were falling behind at every level in school. The code-red subtext, of course, was that young girls are in ascendance. Say it isn't so! It actually wasn't.

Conservative authors had selectively clipped excerpts from an American Association of University Women report about educational disparities for boys and girls based on different races, ethnicities, and income levels and regurgitated their chosen nuggets in books feverishly subtitled *How Misguided Feminism is Harming Our Young Men.* They fed their lines to swarming journalists and they bit. Reporters never read the original text of the AAUW study, and most importantly, they seemed to ignore the fact that men continue to outearn women in the workplace. That is a crisis some girls would love to have.

Besides, in Japan boys go to their rooms; here they seem to go on *American Idol.*

In one very real boy crisis, the sisters Karen, Condi, and Laura Rental have been coaxing young George out of his weight room, giving him DVD highlight reels of hurricanes, the Cuban baseball crisis, and PhotoShopped pictures of Jack Abramoff without him. The war is over and he is the last to know. At this rate, I will be in my nineties before George comes stumblebumbling out of an island gated community, waving a tiny white flag. Karl Rove will already have given the camera position instructions from his cell.

............................................................................

# Mashups and Me

### March 2006

I have not spent a lot of time down at the Genius Bar at the Mac Store of Life, but I am all about the mashups. Started as digitally mixed songs in the pop music world, mashups have now jumped platforms into video. They seamlessly combine disparate content from more than one source into an integrated experience. I am working on several mashup montages, but since I have been on hold with my AOL support representative for three days—and I blame Mary Cheney—I am just going to have to describe them to you.

*Pimp My President:* Hair wisps spiked into a Mohawk, shining gold tooth and elephant bling, Karl Rove rocks the West Wing to the lyrics of "It's Hard Out Here for a Pimp": "With the Cadillac and gas money spent, you got a whole lot of bitches jumpin' ship." Holy Valerie Plame! In the background, Condi in her dominatrix boots works a shredder as the Jack Abramoff Dancers in black fedoras busta move. The alien warship from Independence Day suddenly roosts on the White House. Too late, Karl notices a shadow on his BlackBerry. Kaboom!

*Crouching Blogger, Hidden Slacker:* The Japanese face a crisis with *hikikomori.* Meanwhile, American boys work out their stress issues by night-crawling in their Beemers and paying homeless guys to beat each other up. It's East meets West! A video game is in the works.

*Trans-American League of Their Own:* The *L Word*'s sultry boi Moira injects "T" and morphs into surly man Max. Baseball's Barry Bonds injects steroids—excuse me, flaxseed oil—and goes from San Francisco Giant to Really Giant. A hitting montage: Max hits Jenny, Barry hits baseballs. Fans are sad: Jenny's distraught at her FTM. Our sporty president is upset at his MVP. In spring training Bonds tries to come back with a medley as an oversized Paula Abdul. He still gets booed on the playing field. And the L girls are maxed out on Max. Yer out!

*Blazing Brokeback:* Not that we need another one, but I am working on a mashup of *Brokeback Mountain* and *Blazing Saddles.* I am going straight to the obvious scene of Ennis, Jack, Bart, Jim (the Waco Kid), and Mongo all sitting around the campfire, eating beans from a red lacquered Le Creuset Dutch oven. Mongo tells Ennis to quit mumbling. You know what happens next.

Also in the works if I ever get out of AOL hell: *Oprah's Gonna Blow!*—Oprah bug-eyeing "You lied to me" to Samuel Alito at his Supreme Court confirmation hearing as he bleats, "I didn't mean what I wrote." And *Good Will Hunting*—expert hunter Duck! Cheney shoots his friend in the face and then, like all good hunters, eats him and shares what he doesn't eat with the rest of the village. I just might mash them all up into *A Million Little Lying Pieces.*

·····················································································

# He-Who

### June 2006

The credits rolling after the 1990 Kevin Costner oeuvre *Dances with Wolves* featured the following character names: He who smiles a lot, He who has wind in his hair, She who stands with a fist. Costner's main squeeze, Mary McDonnell, should have been called She who has capped teeth.

All people in the news now sound like the cast from *Dances with Wolves II.* In one *Newsweek* article about NSA wiretapping, five appositional disclaimers were cited to describe some of the characters: He who declined to be named talking about the former director, He who did not want to be named talking about internal matters, He who asked not to be named because of the matter's sensitivity, He who would not be named talking about agency procedures, He who would not speak about internal matters on the record.

Perhaps the He-whos down in Whoville are Bush nicknamery in long form, or perhaps they are observant members of an anonymous

program to which George does not belong, but the final effect is that the Rove-cone of silence makes us all guess workers. Who are these people?

When our nation's high school newspaper, *USA Today,* claimed to break the NSA story, I pored over its pie charts as if they were some recently discovered ancient cuneiform of a civilization I barely knew. But first I tried to cancel Verizon, they who "never stop working for you"—and for the NSA, apparently. They never got back to me. They were too busy digging their data mines. That explains all the Verizon repair huts on the streets of New York. If Al-Qaeda calls, the NSA wants to know who they are talking to. Please leave your number, even if you think we have it. George (He who says they are not listening, just looking for patterns) Bush is resolute. Maybe I will try not paying my bill, just using their service. Can you hear me now?

Then I went back to deciphering the American people. "Based on what you have heard or read about the NSA database of Americans' phone records, do you approve or disapprove of this government program?" Only 51 percent said they disapproved! Forty-three percent approved and 6 percent had no opinion.

"If you knew that the federal government had your telephone records, how concerned would you be?" Forty-four percent would not be concerned at all. This must be the Upright Unconcerned Citizen Brigade—you know, the folks who console themselves with the trope/ tripe "If you don't have anything to hide, you don't have to worry." The breakdown of my fellow concerned citizens was 20 percent "not too," 13 percent "somewhat," and 22 percent "very." One percent had no opinion or perhaps no phone.

While 33 percent of concerneds could not work up a good head of steam about the whole thing, in my household we are reevaluating our all-access pass to the grid because it goes both ways. We have cut up our special-shopper bar code cards. No more online shopping for us. I am looking at my iPod differently. I am swearing off iTunes. The TiVo's got to go. String and tin cans from our home terror kit stash of deviled hams will have to do.

And when I am flying in a full plane, I pretend that rows one through seventeen are that unconcerned 44 percent. I spend the whole flight guessing who they are, and how do they do that?

# The Body Politic

## March 2007

During our long domestic and international nightmare, it is perhaps no mistake that millions of people have paid money to determine their "personal sleep number." By inputting height, weight, mattress preference, and sleep pattern data, trained professionals have helped the sleeplessly addled determine the key to a perfect night's sleep. It is not clear whether George has availed himself of the technology, but he has said, "I'm sleeping better than people would assume." Some assume it was passing out.

Perhaps more noteworthy than the upsurge of sleep numerology in these last years of the Bush administration is the intriguing phenomenon of the traveling exhibit known as Body Worlds. In the last two years, millions of people in the United States have attended sold-out exhibitions of human bodies and body parts preserved and frozen in various poses through a process called plastination. Gunther von Hagens, a German anatomist, invented the technique, put the show on the road, and put me off rocky road Häagen-Dazs for a while.

The stated purpose of Body Worlds is the "education of the layman about the human body leading to better health awareness." Thus the compare-and-contrast exhibit of the smoker's and nonsmoker's lungs, the freestanding circulatory system. The Swimmer, the Archer, the Equestrian, and the Pregnant Woman and her eight-month fetus are some of the more popular displays.

Given the accessibility of these dire dioramas, it is beyond sad irony that we are kept from seeing the unplastinated bodies of our dear soldiers returning from war zones. Embedded photographers are not allowed to take pictures of dead or wounded soldiers. Photos of flag-draped coffins are also forbidden. Because of this de facto censorship, the miseducation of the layman about the impact of the war on our soldiers' actual young bodies continues.

Full disclosure: I have not attended Body Worlds. At first, whenever I saw the ads for the show, I mistakenly dismissed them as movie promos for *Matrix IV*, with a filleted, bug-eyed, crouching Keanu Reeves. A surprising residual reverence for the body as Temple of the Holy Ghost keeps me away.

It cannot be pure sensationalism that drives people to the exhibit. Since most science has been transformed into political science, people want information. We used to just call it general science or biology. Now it is all multiple-choice.

Word has it that when George W. Bush is not deciding to surge, or bullying surge protectors in Congress, he has been ruminating about his legacy. Southern Methodist University, whose motto is the unintentionally ironic "The Truth Shall Set You Free," is the proposed and reluctant site of the Bush II Library: a half-stack of unreadable, blackened FOIA-vetted documents, leather-bound copies of *My Pet Goat*, the French existentialists, and "some Shakespeares." Go, Mustangs! What a Liebrary!

The money could more suitably be spent on the GWB Fitness Center.

Or on a GWB Body Worlds show? They are generally moneymakers, but W. can run anything into the ground in a few short years. We would select different personalities from the Bush years, determine their perfect sleep number, induce a state of even more suspended animation, and put them in dramatic poses. The War Criminal/Adviser (with Henry Kissinger, we would not have to do much). The Anonymous Source. The Retired Military General. The Political Director. The Devoted Personal Assistant/Supreme Court Nominee. The Mother (at last Barbara would be silent). The Hunter. The Hunter's Friend. Look! That's actual buckshot in his face!

We could authorize a traveling road show and, if we run out of sleepinates, dip into the reserve of actual dead people. Ken Lay could at last be a cooperative witness as Corporate CEO. If this gives you a creepy, quasi-necrophiliac feeling, you do not have to attend. But it could keep them all from starting their own consulting firms.

......................................................................................

# Hairspray

## July 2007

Bear Week is over in Ptown. So if you go down to the woods today, you are going to be on your own. I am one sad lesbruin.

After I took the food down from where I had tied it out of the bears' reach, I took to my couch. That is how I happened to watch Renée Zellweger in one of those *Bridget Jones Diarrhea*s. In her real-life, form-fitting fat suit, she predated Edna Turnblad in *Hairspray* and Eddie Murphy in a fat *Norbit* suit, so offensive it cost him the Oscar. Hey, it was raining, Netflix does not come out this far, and our one movie theater in town has been turned into a crepe place, which I attacked on Bastille Day just because. And since when did weight gain pass for acting? Thanks a lotta, Mr. LaMotta.

Because it was so excruciating to watch Zellweger/Jones desperately seeking suitors, I flicked between her and Tom Cruise, the handsome, sofa-hopping Scientologist, in *Minority Report,* a sci-fi flick in which Tom plays a D.C. cop in a precrime unit. Based on intel from precogs floating in a sensory deprivation tank, Tom arrests people before they commit a crime. How to try them if they did not commit a crime? Now you know where Alberto "Gonzo" Gonzales got the idea for Guantánamo.

That filmic afternoon gave me the idea to write a review of the transgenre *Hairspray,* the movie-based-on-the-Broadway-play-based-on-the-movie. Dramamine drip, please. Of course, I could have just written a prereview. Prereviewing is a time-honored tradition among right-wing conservatives. They write reviews without the inconvenience of actually having to see the movie. Think precrime. But the rain had stopped.

Even though I knew I would probably have to view the film on a blueberry crepe, I rode my bike down to our local creperie/theater. I could hardly get across the huge picket line. Kidding. The *Washington*

*Blade* had called for a *Hairspray* boycott because of John Travolta's membership in the "Church" of Scientology. The *Blade* said we should boycott because of L. Ron Hubbard's antigay rhubarbs and because the "church" funds reparative therapies for gays. I remember no similar call to boycott Tom Cruise in *Minority Report,* or I never would have watched. Based on Tracy Turnblad's passion for integration, the KKK, not the gays, should boycott *Hairspray.* Tracy would be undeterred by the Supreme Court's back-to-segregation decision.

In most press junket interviews, Travolta said he is not playing a gay character and Scientology is not homophobic. Therefore it is so. He said he wanted the challenge of playing Edna so that the audience would just see Edna, a vulnerable, voluptuous housewife gone to flesh, and not John Travolta being amazing. Travolta also pointed out that he was not like Robin Williams playing a guy playing Mrs. Doubtfire who actually looked like Glenn Close in the Greta Cammermeyer story. Nor was he like Dustin Hoffman in *Tootsie.* Hoffman, Williams, and Travolta always seem assured that they make better women than women ever do. Mary Martin in *Peter Pan* was my first butch role model, and she never gave off that annoying vibe.

I should have gone with my default movie and watched my personal copy of *Napoleon Dynamite* for the *n*th time. I am learning his "Vote for Pedro" dance. FYI: You cannot do that *Saturday Night Fever* disco thing in moonboots.

· · · · · · · · · · · · · · · · · · · · · · · · · · · · · · · · · · · · · · · · · · · · · · · · · · · · · · · ·

# Dog Days of Summer
## August 2007

Have you tried the three-dimensional thesaurus? You probably have been using it for years, but I just recently discovered it. To find a synonym, you type in the word you need some others for, press Enter, and faster than even Google can congratulate itself, a very space-age,

beautiful floating word map appears like an answer in an upended eight ball.

The 3-D thesaurus looks like a word Tinkertoy with the key word on the center sprocket with spokes to other words. But I think there might be lead paint on it. I already had to ditch my Lead Barbie by Mattel. That kind of wordcentric architectural construct is what it would take to diagram the events of this summer. I have tried a linear description to make sense of it, but it looks like one of my grade-school sentence diagrams, with adverbs dangling off adverbs like some mutant creeping vine.

The word at the center of the construct you need to Venn this late August is "dog." As in dog days of summer. Off that would be the Michael Vick dogfighting/gambling spoke. Barry Bonds must be relieved to have the spotlight off him. Vick admitted to running dog-fights and to inhumane treatment of dogs in his care. In a dyslexic moment of atonement, he said he had found God. He could go to jail, and his days of dogleg right quarterbacking for the Atlanta Falcons seem to be numbered. He would have received no time if he had just modeled himself after another football player and killed his ex-wife. He might even have gotten a book deal.

The understandable revulsion over the canine mistreatment suggests that news coverage of the war, floods, and scandals should focus on dogs to get people riled up. Dogs are dying in Darfur! Dogs do not have basic health care! Dogs were disenfranchised in Florida! The dogs of war are fighting a losing cause in Iraq! It seems to get people's attention. Mitt Romney's family vacation saga and mistreatment of the family's beloved Irish setter would be a way into the story of his former Idaho campaign manager, the foot-tapping, non-gay Republican senator, that old dog Larry Craig.

Just as the Dick Cheney Buckshot Lunch incident lost its absolute last shred of funny, along came Craig's list of hilarious hypocrisy. During June, aka Gay Pride Month, Senator Craig was picked up for lewd behavior in a bathroom at the airport in Minneapolis, the site of next year's Republican convention, if they have one. In our house, we think Dick Cheney is just going to declare himself the candidate. Larry Craig's version of Dick Cheney's famous line, "I just had a beer at lunch," is "I've got a wide stance in a bathroom and my foot might

have grazed the officer in the stall next to mine." Ooftah! P.S. Larry's drag name is Miss Construe.

Another spoke of "dog" would be the Alberto Gonzales resignation. Although Gonzales submitted his resignation on a Friday, the story was released during Vick's Monday press conference. Gonzales, described as "the dogged defender of Bush," wrote the rules of torture, some involving dogs on leashes, and was Bush's lapdog at the Justice Department. Gonzales's hangdog announcement was in contrast to Karl Rove's. With his master smiling his unconditional love behind him, Rove, top dog, announced he was leaving to spend more time with his family. Which was last seen running from the house. Chinese dog-food inspectors at least have the decency to kill themselves when things go wrong. Rove took a victory lap on the Sunday morning Kennel Club shows. He said he was like Moby Dick. The Moby is silent.

Your president, George Bush, once said that his is a lonely job, that at the end of the day all that is left is him and his little black dog, Barney. Where is Laura? Has she left the family to spend more time in politics?

...............................................................................................

# See Alice?

### January 2008

The brilliant journalist Barbara Ehrenreich opined recently and hilariously, "With all the talk about how to stimulate it, you'd think that the economy is a giant clitoris." She says in "Clitoral Economics" that the challenge for the Fed's Ben Bernanke is "how best to get the economy engorged and throbbing again."

Ain't gonna happen with that stubbly beard.

While the island of Manhattan fantasizes itself the epicenter of the financial world and does indeed look clitoral nestled between the vulvar folds of New Jersey and Long Island, this economy has nothing to do with that sweet bud of pleasure.

This economy, shrunken from an addiction to the steroids of tax cuts, a dependence on the Acujack of subprime mortgages and the Viagra of war spending, is more penile than clitoral. How is that for a gender card? And what goes up must come down. Except that we have been the main party animal/sex addict at the global orgy, and when we step out of the daisy chain to get some lube or take a nap, everybody gets freaked.

This is so much fun. I've got a million of 'em. Is that a stimulus package or are you just happy to see me? You know the wide-stance joke is coming. If it's been up more than four years, call your doctor.

Unless it is President Curveball. Instead of putting money into unemployment insurance, or into states to help them balance budgets, which they must do, unlike some people I know, George is giving everybody a parting rebate check, as if it is his money he is throwing around. And he is giving that post-9/11 spiel about going out and buying more mountains of things. It's patriotic.

Sometimes I do not know whether to laugh, cry, or burn the furniture.

······································

# Crabby Putinesca
## April 2008

It is an amazing spring day here in New York City. Finally. The trees are leafing out, providing cover for the tattered plastic Fairway bags lufting all winter in the bare tree branches. The yellow forsythia petals have given way to green leaf. The jonquils are past. But it is high bloom time for the flowering crab apple trees in Riverside Park. I wish I could freeze-frame them, but their mutability is their poignant charm.

To reverse one of my favorite literature tropes, that old pathetic fallacy of the personification of inanimate objects, allow me to floral-

ize myself. This long primary season, I am one flowering crab, but without the charm.

As the postprimary letdown sets in in Pennsylvania and Keystone Staters get back to actual bitterness, Indiana and North Carolina are now in the media spotlight. The big Good Sam Club RV map of where we have been will have the last magnetized states of West Virginia, Kentucky, Oregon, South Dakota, and Montana all filled in by June 3. And then the gas-guzzling behemoth of the Democratic Party will trundle off to Colorado, the Rocky Mountain State, and Denver.

Donner, party of one.

Unlike many of my friends, I am not cranky that the race goes on. I am not calling for Hillary to leave the race or for Bill to leave the human race. Okay, maybe the latter. I remind my impatient friends, this too is what democracy looks like. They have not seen it for seven and a half years, so they are confused.

What I am most crabby appleton about is the media coverage:

John King obsessively poking his military-inspired voting GPS system as Wolf looks on over his shoulder, slack-jawed, like a Cro-Magnon discovering fire.

Furrow-browed and deeply caring Reverend Bill Moyers hearing Jeremiah Wright's confession.

Mary Matalin—not Marlee Matlin, who cannot hear, but the Matalin who does not listen—tight-lipping her theory that the Democrats really do not want to win the White House. They are more concerned with solidifying their hold on Congress. They could care less.

Well, I do not care what Democrat wins the presidency; I just want her to appoint me as media czar. And I do not mean that namby-pamby kind of czar Bush appoints when he has no clue what to do. War czar, for example. The place should be crawling with Katrina czars, Gitmo czars, subcrime mortgage czars. I mean the old Russian crabby czars. Like Putin.

In one of their first meetings, Bush and Putin apparently had one of those middle-school staring contests. George looked into Putin's eyes and pronounced he saw a good soul. Putin looked into George's eyes and saw directly to the back of his head. When the story broke that Putin was having an affair with a Russian Olympian, a gold medalist in rhythmic gymnastics, he was asked about it at a press confer-

ence. His wife did not appear at his side. Putin, he of the good soul, waxed on creepily about how Russian women are the best, Italians second, and then groused about people with "infected noses" who dig into other people's private lives. Which was how he got his start.

The next day the reporter's paper was shut down. The picture of the pretzel-like gymnast with the sole of her foot on the back of her head disappeared. No word on the poor guy who asked the question at the press conference.

That kind of media czar, but maybe a little less gulagy. I would institute mandatory term limits on all pundits. Race and gender parity must be observed in rehiring. I would make it illegal to use your own name in the title of a news show. I would institute restraining orders on bloggers. They are not allowed to blog unless they can verify that they have left the house that day and made eye contact with and spoken to three actual people. Every Blog-Free Friday they must step away from their vehicles. They must wear actual clothes, not pajamas, to blog.

I am hoping Rachel Maddow will agree to be my deputy czar.

# Sister Friends

The sexism of the Obama-Clinton primary threw me back to my old radical lesbian feminist separatist days. And when I say sexism, someone always inserts, "There was racism too." No doubt about it. Discussing sexism does not negate racism. One implies and abets the other. Ditto class, age, and abilities, while we are at it. Eight years of Bush and no one can hold even two thoughts anymore. Multitasking, applauded in all other areas of life, is not valued in multithinking. It was past time for a reunion of my old Urban Lesbian Swat Team. I read the minutes of our old CR meetings. Arm every straight woman. Give lesbians the bullets. We would work together. Wives are property. Property is theft. It's not all men, but it's always men. We were so Old Testament. I made plans to get off the grid. Commandeer an Olivia cruise boat. Sail away. But I did not want to miss the last half-season of *The L Word*.

# Feeling Potlucky

## June 2005

I love Pride Month and all, but in recent years it has been missing something: the lesbian potluck. Late last year, to mark my girlfriend's return to health, I decided to revive that old custom.

When we invited some friends who had not come up or out in the lesbian separatist ranks—either because they had come out late in life or because they were too young—they were nervous. Yes, even though they were accomplished professionals and slick post-chic L's, they were intimidated by our little potluck.

I explained that years ago, when lesbians were isolated and invisible, potlucks were a way to build community. I reassured them that I would guide them through the ancient potluckian rituals: their choice of flannel (no pinks), the pheromonic properties of patchouli, and the uses of tofu.

We gathered, happy to see each other, giving actual hugs instead of instant-message greetings or voices left on answering machines. We realized that though we had been in cybercontact, we had not been in actual physical contact. I had made deft food group assignments, and our guests fulfilled them brilliantly. Always ask the Libra couple to bring dessert. They could not decide and so brought a dessert dim sum. After the main dish of dish, the conversations flowed from film to nanotechnology, nonmonogamy, art, same-old-sex marriage, the patriarchy. After so many dinners ruined during that fall's political season by someone banging her forehead on the table moaning "Whadderwegonnado?" it was a bracing, fun night.

We had another potluck on International Women's Day, March 8. Magnifique! Again it was as if we had suddenly returned from a nightmarish, not-so-rapturous journey to a promised land of cybercommunity. The food, the arm resting on a friend's shoulder, the heat—all grounded us.

We scheduled our next potluck for Mother's Day. The expanded list was too big for our place, so we cheated, called it a "nouveau potluck," and met at a restaurant. Again the hugging, the kissing, the mighty real. Again the catch-up, the dish, the wide-ranging discussions and disagreements. Lesbians were switching seats like musical chairs, joining in true pods, not iPods, of laughing, yakking, and eating.

At about 9:40 p.m., when things were loud and cranking, I sensed a weird shift in energy. Some lesbians were motioning for checks, slinging on backpacks—decamping. I asked one tall young friend, "You leaving?" She nodded sheepishly. "Another event?" I asked. Again the sheep. They were going over to her place to watch *The L Word.* "You're going to watch virtual lesbians and miss these actual lesbians?" A slug of Woolite. Another nod and a backing out of the door.

Diminished, we, the left-behind, sat with empty glasses and half-eaten tarts. We wondered why they could not watch the rerun at eleven. Didn't they have TiVo? What were we, chopped lesbian liver?

I am not giving up. Our next potluck is a summer solstice picnic. It is on a Saturday. Softball is mandatory. Bring a mitt.

......................................................................................

# King of My Heart
## July 2006

As the deciderator in chief leads us down the abyss and misfortune continues to hump our leg, I have been thinking about leadership.

For me it is a cardio thing. My dear girlfriend gave me the latest iPod in the fond hope that I would get off the eight-track and onto the treadmill. I have 186 songs so far. It is the audio books I love. At the gym, I have listened to books about the leaders George Washington, Abraham Lincoln, and Martin Luther King. While others on their treadmills pop to hip-hop, I have been known to stop and shriek like

some Paula Revere, "The British have taken New Jersey!" before I fly off the back end of the treadmill.

As more and more retired military generals reveal the arrogant lack of preparedness and "strategery" of Rumsfeld and his boys, I sound like Joan Cusack from *In & Out,* screaming at Kevin Kline after he tells her he is gay at their wedding: "Was there, oh, any other time you might have told me this?"

For real leadership, I think I prefer the King. Billie Jean, that is.

And let me just catch my breath, as I realize that in five days HBO aired almost seven hours about powerful, real women. Where are my smelling salts?

Though HBO's *Billie Jean King: Portrait of a Pioneer* had a bit too much of her ex, Larry King (not the one with suspenders and the extra row of bottom teeth) for my taste, it gave us the best portrait yet of how Billie Jean got to be the leader she is today. By seeing the scope of what she has done over the years, we can all take some leadership pointers from her life story.

*Lead from where you are and from what you love.* Billie worked for equal pay for women in tennis, the game she loved, with the same brilliant, competitive strategy she used on the court.

*Reach out to your rivals as assets and allies.* Billie saw that the new darling of tennis, Chris Evert, could help her quest to popularize women's tennis as a legitimate contender in the sports world.

*Admit your mistakes.* Billie admitted, in what must have been an excruciating press conference, that, yes, she had had an affair with a woman when she was married. Then she went back to work.

*Make connections.* Billie never fails to connect race and class with gender as a practical matter of justice.

*Keep your message simple.* Billie's definition of feminism as "equality for girls and boys" cuts through acres of ridicule and verbiage. Since we all need to rethink and retool our strategies for achieving full LGBT equality, one of my favorite Kingisms is "Champions adjust."

Once when I was whining to Billie about some new show I was struggling with, she quietly reminded me, "Kate, pressure is a privilege."

Lead on, my King! And damned be he who first cries, "Hold, enough!"

## Desperate Housewiles

### December 2006

Now that the election is over—oh, my God, more on that another time—I can get back to thinking about marriage in New Jersey. The New Jersey Supreme Court left us hanging. No reason to deny us legal union, they ruled. But what should our unions be called? The New Jersey legislature gets to fight that out.

Well, I am nothing if not civic, so I consulted my inner pollster. What word would get our positives up and our negatives down? I wanted a word for marriage that was values-neutral. Perhaps something from a food group—Cinnabon? Everyone loves Cinnabon! Something that represented our conflicted feelings on marriage—those who can, care less; those who can't, care more.

Here is what I realized. Our enemies are right: there is no other word for marriage. So let's keep the word but put it in quotes to represent all our ambivalences. From now on, I think it should be mandatory to do those double-pumped bunny ears with your fingers in the air every time you say the *m* word or any of its variants. We got "married." She asked me to "marry" her. If you do not pump, it is a felony punishable by reading Mary Cheney's book.

Whatever you call it, Oprah will not do it. After she established her "just friends" cred with Gayle, for the tedious *n*th time, Oprah felt confident enough to do a show on lesbians coming out of "marriage" to men. Apparently these women were so pretty, people complained that they could not have been lesbians. One of my favorite lesbophobic tropes. Listen, after what happened to Oprah with James Frey, I am sure each lesbianic background was completely fact-checked. And I would have liked that job.

Despite Oprah's breathless ratings-driven attention to this phenomenon, it is really quite old and ordinary. Like me. In the early 1980s I was performing in Ohio and staying in community housing.

Unlike more marginal, earnest, crunchy-granola billeting, this was a solid upper-middle-class suburban house in a very straight neighborhood far from the homo-heights gay section of town. One of the women had been "married" to a man and had gotten the house in the divorce. After some wine, over an unapologetically meaty, wheat-laden meal, she regaled us with stories of the neighborhood.

Imagine the voiceover for Wisteria Lane as a very randy, mischievous lesbian. Talk about desperate housewives. The women got the children off to school, hung out at one of their pools, paired off, and were back before everyone came home. Things were especially busy on warm summer nights—they had an elaborate system of lights to indicate when someone was available. This was years before Melissa Etheridge sang, "Come to My Window." My new friend said that on a family trip to the Magic Kingdom, one of the women had shagged the girl in the Peter Pan costume.

When you realize that even same-old-sex "marriage" is really a secret gateway to lesbianism, you begin to see the Right's paranoia. No wonder they call Ohio a battleground state.

......................................................................

# Tant P.U.

## May 2007

In France, Monsieur Sarkozy defeated Madame Royal, and I am trying not to read into that defeat the defeat of Madame Hillary Clinton. Just in case I was having an easy time keeping them separate, along came Maureen Dowd to relink the two. Apparently Maureen, who never met a powerful woman she didn't like to slice and dice, had been going a little too heavy with her Hillary-hating and so went to France to find a stunt double. Voilà Royal!

No one has ever damned a woman with such faint praise so cleverly as that nutty *New York Times* redhead, who, when it comes to

keeping women down, answers her own book title question, "Are men necessary?" To keep women down? No need, answers Maureen, I'll do it for you.

Nicolas Sarkozy, the feisty, energetic son of an immigrant, which entitles him to call other immigrants scum, wants to reinvigorate France's economy and restore its alliance with America. To do the economy part, he has to get the giant Airbus of their economy off the ground, and that means getting the French off the thirty-five-hours-a-workweek dole. The French voted not only for a longer workweek but also for le petit's Napoleonic manliness. And you thought only Kansans voted against their own interests.

Obviously the Starbucks Enterprise has landed in France and has caffeinated everyone into ma vie en venti-sized guilt. When history is written, it will be revealed that Starbucks was a corporate conspiracy to get everyone to work longer hours. I have friends who wearily proclaim, "I worked eighty-seven hours last week." C'est pathétique. In Japan, overwork is now a felony.

The same week Sarkozy and his right-to-work-long-hours won in France, Ellen DeGeneres did a week of shows from her hospital bed on set. It was not even sweeps week. DeGeneres had reached down to pick something up at home and torn something in her back and was doctor-ordered to complete bed rest. Her work ethic made her go on with the show. The painkillers helped.

It was also about job security. In case you were wondering if women on TV are worried about their hard-won jobs, even Ellen DeGeneres seemed insecure about her job if she was out for a week. I bet Johnny Carson never worried that someone sitting in for him would take over his job. Joan Rivers looked too eager and they squashed her like a bug. How do you say *reruns* en français? Ellen could have called a number of other women comics to sit in for her. I can dance. It was a plucky performance but a little sad to see. The good news is that it inadvertently demonstrated that Americans really do not care what lesbians do in bed. As long as they do their job.

························································································

# Kiss My Benchmark

## May 2007

Last weekend I was sitting in my old Jeep in a parking lot at a seafood stand in Ptown, waiting for a friend to get the world's most expensive, smallest lobster roll. The place was packed. The lobster roll was not. I was listening to *A Prairie Home Companion* and its special Memorial Day show from Wolf Trap, outside Washingtoons, D.C. Ever since Garrison Keillor tried to blog funny about gay men adopting children, I have been a little reluctant to listen. And sometimes his breathy voice is a little too pervy for me.

But the music was heartbreakingly tender ballads of leaving loved ones behind to fight the great big last war to end all wars. The finality of those separations is contrasted with the global connectedness of this war through e-mails, podcasts, and Skype phones. Yet the pain of physical separation—"I'll be seeing you in all the old familiar places," "What'll I do when you are far away?"—is just as real now for young soldiers and their families.

As I listened, absentmindedly watching all the sunburned people returned from the beach, I got all choked up, so I went home and called my oldest brother. He had been drafted, learned Vietnamese at the ironically named Fort Bliss, Texas, and served a year in Vietnam. His job was interpreter with the pacification troops, who went into towns and villages to help with rebuilding. He did not talk about it when he got home, except for one story about almost falling out of a helicopter making a quick exit from a village that was not quite ready to be rebuilt. We caught up a bit on his family's Memorial Day picnic plans and then I thanked him for serving in Vietnam. He was quiet, then said, "That is so weird. You're the second person to thank me. Back then, no one thanked us."

Sometimes it is surreal to be in a vacation town as the world goes to hell around us. Like during this dirge of a surge. Just a few streets

away on Commercial, the town was filling with fabulous young lesbians from colleges all over the Northeast on one last huge fling. Ptown is an unofficial party stop on the unofficial lesbian party circuit. I interviewed some of them—that is what I'm calling it, anyway—and they said it is all word of mouth. And a lovely mouth it is.

Speaking of mouths, I will miss Rosie's mouth on *The View*. There are certainly different ways of fighting the war, and she chose to be outspoken and unwilling to swallow the extraordinary renditions from the Bush "administration" about what is happening. For that she was treated as a big hysterical lesbian. Interesting how the other side does an operation distraction and focuses on the girlfight and not the war. I hope she has a good summer rest and comes back on her own late-night show.

Midst the constant coverage of Lindsay Lohan's last fling, I saw the story that Cindy Sheehan, mother of a son killed early on in the war, announced that she is depleted from fighting the administration and her so-called allies. She is going home. She should rest and come back as Rosie's sidekick. Let's all rest up this summer, because come September, they can kiss my benchmark.

...........................................................................................................

# You Logo, Girl!
## August 2007

Could I possibly be more jaded? The Democratic presidential candidates made time in their multiformatted debating/campaigning/fundraising schedules to debate on, as the other cable-anchorites called it, "Logo, the gay-themed cable channel." And I was all ho-hum.

It took me an ungrateful minute, but that was awesome! Holy Yes I Am, Batgirl! It is 2007 and we have a ding-dang gay channel and the Dems debated on it. We took our rightful place with YouTube questioners, blogging conventioneers, whooping AFL-CIOers on steam-

ing hot Soldiers Field. Next stop, the Food Channel. Would you ban transfats in Oreos? Discuss.

Despite dire, bogus Fox News warnings that it is a known fact that candidates who align themselves with gay groups do not do well in elections and develop hardened facial boils and a propensity for lattes, those otherwise chickenshit-cannot-defeat-a-wiretapping-bill-before-recess Democrats did due diligence and appeared on Logo.

The Republican primates did not even return Logo's calls (no insult meant to primates). Their lowly staff minions, often closeted gay preppies, sneered "As if . . ." at the invitation to participate.

Not only did the Dems debate, they struggled with their answers. It was painful/fun to watch them twitch and spin their desire to get rid of "don't ask, don't tell," their love for their gay friends and family, their support for workplace nondiscrimination, and then try to square all that goodwill with their logic-defying lack of support for gay marriage. We are used to the liberal, secular version of "love the sinner, hate the sin." I do hope some straight folks were watching. Some candidates—okay, Hillary Clinton—seemed particularly cautious and aware that anything she said would be an ominous tagline in a Republican campaign ad in about ten minutes.

We will see if the candidates are as gay-forthcoming in nongay formats, but I wish one of the gay inquisitors (We had gay inquisitors! Oh, how our place at the table has turned!) had asked them if they thought heterosexuality was a choice or biological. Why not ask straight people if they think being heterosexual is a choice? It seems to be their area of expertise. The real question is not whether homosexuality is a choice or biological but why it is so stigmatized. I did not mind Bill Richardson's answer at all. I do mind him. He said he thought being gay was a choice. I am pro-choice all the way. Being a lesbian is the choicest choice a gal can make.

As I redden at my own jaded ho-humming this morning, I am receiving excited e-mails about the departure of Karl Rove, who announced that he is leaving his post as presidential adviser to spend more time with his family. Which was last seen running screaming from the house. Some posit hopeful scenarios that finally the Dems are going to nail him. Oh, please. They are hapless. And Dick Cheney is still running things, getting ready to declare martial law and his

preemptive presidency. Karl Rove is figuring out how to spin that scenario right now. I think I am beginning to identify the source of all my jade.

But that night on Logo was still gob-smackingly awesome. And not just because it was not another rerun of *Priscilla, Queen of the Desert*.

...........................................................................................................

# This One's for You, Mildred
### October 2007

For those of you breathlessly waiting to update my where- and how-abouts, with your pushpins suspended over your darling homemade Kate Clinton tour maps, I apologize for my tardy check-in. Your arms must be sore. You know who you are. Mildred W. in Sioux Falls.

The reason for my silence is quite simple: the collapse of the Mets. I mean, I knew that the bee colony collapse, which I have been following and chronicling for you—a bit obsessively, some would say—signaled the beginning of other collapses—bridges, mines, the dollar, Oral Roberts University—but the Mets were way ahead of their division with just two weeks to go and they did not even make the wild-card draw. Never has any team in baseball suffered such a precipitous end-of-the-season collapse.

I have no idea what I am talking about. I am merely parroting the ESPN chatter. It is the only thing I can safely watch on television without mild panic attacks. Rachel Ray gives me agita. It is like she ate Suze Orman. Did you know that those big-necked sportscasters say basically the same thing hour after hour with maybe a few new scores here and there? They are very convincing in their endless enthusiasm. Does anyone ever randomly test them for performance-enhancement drugs? I bet BALCO delivers.

Speaking of which, I love Marion Jones. Now more than ever. She

made an apology that was clearer than her clear and should be a template for all other apologies that we will never hear from Bonds, McGwire, etc. I knew she was roiding back at the Olympics, but my feeling was, give her more and see how fast that gal can really go. Whining George Vecsey, eat my dust.

About that pushpin. I had the complete pleasure of appearing in D.C. with Norman Lear's advocacy group, People For the American Way, for its Liberty Awards. Richly deserved honors were given at the Kennedy Center to the entrepreneurial philanthropist Tim Gill; the documentarians of *Jesus Camp*, Heidi Ewing and Rachel Grady; the Rutgers women's basketball coach, C. Vivian Stringer; and Madame Speaker of the House, California's gift to double-knits, Representative Nancy Pelosi.

While I was onstage, I got the international symbol for "keep talking" from the show's producer, Joel Silberman, because the Speaker was still on the hill trying to get the State Children's Health Insurance Program bill passed. It passed. George vetoed it, saying that we did not have the money for it. That was the same day the Senate approved $459 billion for war spending. I want my ESPN.

A few days later I had the pleasure of attending the huge Out & Equal Workplace Summit, also in D.C. I attended panels and plenaries and got to hang with the amazing band Betty and to be inspired by Toshi and Bernice Johnson Reagon. The 2,300 attendees were fired up to continue to bring LGBT visibility and equality to their workplaces. I emceed their raucous awards dinner, a celebration of their good work. Justice is good business. Someone tell George.

Today I am gathering up the pinnies and the orange field cones for my annual touch football game at Women's Week. For those of you with your pushpins, Mildred, I will be in Ptown all next week for what we used to call "the Running of the Mullets," but we are way too styling for that kind of talk now.

......................................................................

# Argh, O'Mateys!

## January 2008

Am just back from a lovely Olivia cruise celebrating its thirty-fifth anniversary. Olivia, now a leader in lesbian leisure—a phrase I never thought I would hear or say—began in 1973 as a record label for the unrecorded voices of lesbians. Meg Christian, Cris Williamson, Teresa Trull, and Linda Tillery were just some of the talents Olivia brought to a vibrant lesbian distribution network. In 1988, I emceed the festivities when Olivia celebrated its fifteenth anniversary at Carnegie Hall, and as I walked with cofounder Judy Dlugacz over to the after-party, she said to me, "I'm thinking of doing an Olivia cruise." I thought lesbian cruising sounded redundant, but for twenty years the ships of Olivia have plied the seas and transformed Club Meds throughout the world. Captain Judy is a maritime maven.

Just as Olivia once transformed itself from a record company to a travel company, it continues to change and transform the travel market. There are longer themed cruises—lesbian leadership cruises with Billie Jean King; sports cruises with Cheryl Swoopes and Martina Navratilova; lesbian author cruises with Jewelle Gomez and Katherine V. Forrest; full-frontal fandom cruises with the cast of *The L Word*. Olivia is now developing shorter urban flings to cities like Seattle and Las Vegas for younger, hipper lesbians afraid to leave their desks for very long in this market. For land-based lesbians who love to laugh, there are the popular Comedy Weeks at Club Meds. There, bemused and confused Club Med staffs try to get uninterested lesbians to do the Macarena. In addition to entertainment imports like Cho and Lang, Olivia continues to rely on its beloved and longtime comics—Vicki Shaw, Karen Williams, Suzanne Westenhoefer, Lisa Koch, Roxanna Ward, Amy Boyd, and René Hicks—to keep the party going.

We sailed out of Ft. Lauderdale, where all the older northern gays who can afford it have migrated to. If they do not like it in Florida,

they move to Asheville, North Carolina, and are known there as "halfbacks." Finally, gay halfbacks. We sailed out toward the Turks and Caicos and Tortola, and I jumped ship in St. Maarten. Sad to say, it was a bit rainy and cloudy the days I was on board. I believe it was a low-pressure disturbance from all the hot air coming out of Florida. Buh-bye, Rudy Giuliani!

k.d. lang did a sail-away concert and kicked off the world tour of her new CD, *Watershed*. She absolutely kicked the guts out of a Jane Siberry/Leonard Cohen medley that warmed the hearts of everyone, especially the Canadians. Margaret Cho also did a hysterical set that even bothered me in some sections. That is a good show.

After they jumped ship, we set sail, and though usually I am a good seafarer, I had to take a couple of Bonines, my new drug of choice, to get through my show. It did enhance my performance, but not my memory. The front row, actually a couple of codependent gals from Seattle, were very helpful in keeping me on some kind of track.

The thirty-fifth anniversary cruise was like an old lesbo reunion. Singer and activist Holly Near brought her posse—Adie Torf, musician extraordinaire; Amy Horowitz, founder of Roadwork and Sisterfire; Melissa Howden, Holly's former road manager and documentary filmmaker; Torie Osborne, women's activist and organizer, fresh from being the deputy mayor in L.A. Meg Christian was in the house. Our dinners were raucous—especially after they discovered, to their horror, that I was for Hillary Clinton.

My pal Kate Moira Ryan, who wrote *The Beebo Brinker Chronicles,* a play based on the Ann Bannon lesbian pulp novels of the 1950s, had a little rest before returning to NYC and rehearsals for the show, scheduled to open Off-Broadway, and presented by Lily Tomlin and Jane Wagner.

Thankfully, while we were at sea, I missed the State of the Union address. We are at war, in recession, and the ship of state is taking on water. And that is the good news.

As always, it was great to get a chance to talk to so many women from around the country and the world. And to dance wildly with a bunch of gals, pals old and new. I am the luckiest lesbian. Who could not like walking around hearing, "We love you, Kate"? I asked Kate Ryan, who lives in Brooklyn, if she will come up and tail me as I go

about my day, doing errands, getting stuff for the Super Bowl/Super Tuesday party. She said she would stand on the corner of Seventy-third and Broadway and say, "We love you, Kate!" I promised I would plug her show.

..................................................................................................

# Big Love Trumps Mr. Big
### June 2008

Clinton gals and Obama gals, why can't we all get along?

Let's take a cue from the gals in *Sex and the City*.

You might have missed the opening week of *SATC* because you were consumed with the last installments of *The Sisterhood of the Traveling Pantsuit*. I know I was. But it is hot out. At least go for the air-conditioning. And the pleasure of sitting in a theater packed with 85 percent women and the gay men who love them.

*Iron Man. Indiana Jones.* The dude flicks of summer's standard "women as afterthought" film festivals are usually packed with men and a few of the women who love them. No reviewer ever sniffs about that audience.

The preposterism of the "stylized violence" (whatever that means) of those bummer schlockbusters made passersby in Hartford, Connecticut, fully expect that the hit-and-run victim sprawled before them could get up, dust himself off, and go about his day. They did not need to help out. That is my theory.

As my *SATC* date (with whom, coincidentally, I have same-sex in the city) and I surveyed the satisfied, post-*Sex* women streaming out of the theater in a din of high, happy voices, we both thought, "What a missed organizing opportunity!" NOW should have sign-up tables in all multiplex lobbies. LATER should too.

This Fab Four loves each other! More *Big Love* than Mr. Big. Like

sister-wives without the Mormon front-loaded hair or the prairie dresses. Unless, of course, it was Frontier FLDS Fashion Week in New York.

For such a relentlessly heterosexist chick flick, it was more lesbian than *L Word*. And I love that the lesbian who does not play one in this movie or on TV has the steamiest, most alabaster-skinned, and way too brief sex scene. Cannot wait for the DVD extras.

Yes, they are white and rich. Yes, they marry because they can. Certainly those preconditions can smooth the way for friendship. But sometimes they do not. For Carrie, Samantha, Miranda, and Charlotte, it works because they talk. Male critics say endlessly. The friends speak their unspeakables. They forgive each other. They go on. They are there for each other.

Obama and Clinton gals—let's get it on! And get on with it.

# Ptown GPS

## July 2008

One of the big controversies in Provincetown this summer involves complaints by fifty-third-generation descendants of the Puritans about nudity and public sex in the far reaches of the Herring Cove dunes. The good news is that my worry that gay marriage is a straight conspiracy to stop gay sex is apparently and happily unfounded.

For those of you who would, of course, like to know the exact coordinates of the sexual activity, check your GPS: Gay People Sex. And don't forget: if it's three, let it be. The poison ivy, not the ménages. The poison ivy leaves are just turning a very helpful red alert.

The National Park rangers can divert giant over-sand motor-home behemoths just by putting up the flimsiest of strings and posting PIPING PLOVER NESTING AREA signs. People honor those areas. My suggestion is that the overworked and underpaid civil servants rope off

sexually active areas of the dunes and put up GAY SEX FROLICKING AREA signage. After the initial posting, there would be no need for time-consuming beach patrols.

Everybody sing (to the tune of "Oh, the farmers and the ranchers must be friends), "Oh the gay folks and the Puritans must be friends."

The rangers have better things to do with their time. On a recent high tide, made higher by the pull of a full moon, an elderly woman was stranded on a spit of sand and called for help. One man called the park rangers, who said they were not in the business of rescue. Those trying to be Good Samaritans found another man, with a small rubber dinghy, who was ready to row out to the woman. At that moment the coast guard arrived and would not allow the attempted rescue, because the man did not have enough lifejackets on board.

If only the elderly woman on that tiny strip of sand had stripped naked and done a suggestive hoochee-koo, she would not have had to wait for the ebb tide or suffer from hypothermia.

In international news, Angelina Jolie gave birth to her twins. Mother and children are doing well. Seconds after they were born, the twins were handed to Brad Pitt, who reportedly hugged them to his naked chest. Into the world through Angelina's legs and then placed on Brad's chest! What a charmed life those children already lead! I am happy for them, and yes, just a little jealous.

The Jolie/Pitt blessed event augurs well for the beginning of Gay Family Week here in the town of P. We are just coming to the end of the first ever Girl Splash! Week. Organizers hope that it will grow as big as October's Women's Week. Lynette Molnar says, "In a few more years, we hope it will be like Women's Week but without the Polartec." Pool parties, whale watches, and dance parties were some of the highlights.

I am all set for Family Week. I have rented two Zipkids for four hours a day for the week. I am on a waiting list for what they tell me is a "babe-magnet" adorable six-month-old girl named Karla. My rented double-wide stroller is fully loaded. For me it also doubles as a walker.

Of course, it is wonderful to see rainbow colors of kids in the tiniest colors of the rainbow Crocs you have ever seen. In past Family

Weeks the children seemed to age out at about five and I worried that either the older kids were balking at attending or their parents were turning kids in at a certain age. "Here is a sixteen-year-old. I'll take two eight-year-olds." Every parent is tempted.

But as the Gay Family Week gains history, the most wonderful part of the week is the roving gangs of teen kids of gay parents. They were there all along. They were in organizing workshops sponsored by COLAGE, a national organization for the estimated ten million children of LGBT parents. They are feisty, smart, political, and very fashionable, and they love being with each other. This summer is my eighty-fourth season performing in Ptown. Thanks to their gay parents and COLAGE, the way these kids are maturing, I can retire happily in a few seasons.

# Bawdy Politics

Though I am not bragging, I have bona fide baby-boomer cred. I was born in 1947, the same time as Israel and Pakistan. I have had a much easier time of it. When I tell people I am sixty, they ask my secret. I say, "You are what you eat." They ask if I have had work done. Admittedly I spent a lot of summers on lakes in upstate New York, slathering on baby oil and sitting in aluminum canoes, but no, I have not had work done. If I did, I would send the bill to the White House, because for eight years I have been making a squinting, "What the . . . ?" face and now have a deep Botox-defying furrow circa 2000. People ask if I will continue to work. I worry they know something I do not know. Turning sixty has changed my work life. Fact is, I work well on deadlines. And while my coboomers are working on their bucket lists, I am making a list of things I do not ever want to do again before I die. I do not want to live through another nineteen-month-long presidential campaign. Why start in Iowa? I do not want to have to fight the Title IX fight for sports equality for women again. I do not want to be used as a wedge issue in an election. I do not want to learn how to use a new handheld information system.

# An American Impressionist

## February 2006

Despite a daily, strictly medicinal dose of the *New York Times* cross-word puzzle, I do often draw huge honking blank holes of memory. I used to fight it, but now I embrace it. I might not remember the restaurant, what we ate, or who was there, but I do remember that we had a lovely or dreadful time. Details come, details go, but impressions remain. I am an American impressionist.

It is my twenty-fifth anniversary of performing. I would like to do a few impressions for you.

In the early eighties I did a set at a comedy club in L.A. After, in his dark wood-paneled office, the manager told me, "You can't do that gay stuff." In the late nineties I did another set at that club and a different manager whined, "I thought you were going to do more gay stuff."

At seven a.m. in a tiny, blue-egg-cartoned radio station whose frequency could not have been heard for more than a three-block radius, an interviewer began, "I love your music." I replied, "You hear it too?"

Before I clambered into the huge red boat of a New York Gay Pride grand marshal convertible, I reminded my co-marshal and fellow traveler, the activist, writer, and theologian Father John McNeill, that when he was my college ethics professor, he had huffed wearily that "homosexuality was nothing more than mutual masturbation." As rainbow ribbons snapped in the bright morning around us, I told him that that had set me back a few years. He winced and said, "Please forgive me." I said, "Do not let it happen again, but for your penance you are going to have to ride on the hump."

In Buffalo, New York, where I grew up and still had relatives, the producers did a daring full-frontal job of advertising "the openly lesbian comic" in the local papers. I come from a family of readers. I walked out onstage and there in the third row was my ninety-year-

old Uncle Harold with my seventy-five-year-old Aunt Margie. During the show, Margie seemed to ogle the women around her. I was taken aback, and then I remembered that she was a retired electrologist. Margie had stumbled into a follicular bonanza! The only thing Uncle Harold said to me after the show was "I'm ninety, y' know." But it sounded like "I was seventy-five when I came in, and after what I heard here tonight, I'm ninety now."

At a show in Ottawa, Canada's very federal capital, the producers told me to smile when I left the building because I was being video-taped from a window across the street. This was after a big Canadyke had come up to me and said, "I came because I heard you were a feminist humorist, and if you made fun of us, I was going to punch you out."

One of the best compliments I ever got was after a show in Lexington, Kentucky. The producers had gone all-out. The stage was decorated with huge cardboard Hydrox cookies and tree-trunk-like freestanding tampons. The audience went all-out too. After the show I was having a celebratory repast with the producers and a young dyke came up, gave me a good crack on the back, and proclaimed, "Kate Clinton, you made me want to fuck again."

In a cultural time of discredited memoir and a political time of memory as shredder, it left a lasting impression.

## Not Full Citizens
### October 2006

The New York Supreme Court exhibited classic pre-9/11 thinking in its ruling that the state constitution does not permit gay couples to marry—9/11 B.C. The court's majority referenced sexual preference rather than sexual orientation. They "reasoned" that since same-sex parents do not have children by "accident or impulse," gay parenting is unhealthy for children. This is not a decision. This is a cry for help.

Or maybe they are really just protecting gay couples from the horror that is marriage? Is this the new "closeted tolerance"? I am not a lawyer, but the court's brief made so little sense, I began to worry that my worst fears had been realized. Is it possible that the Domino's Pizza School of Law has graduated its first class and is already fast-tracking them onto the state's highest bench?

Please note that commentators on the cable shows did not sneer endlessly that these are activist judges. No, the New York Supreme Court was just doing the right thing.

Since the decision in our so-called liberal state, I have been trying to rally my fellow gay New Yorkers. Because we are apparently not full citizens of our Empire State, I think we should jaywalk whenever we want. Decline to do jury duty. And I do not think gay people should pay taxes. A friend pointed out that "they" put people in jail for not paying taxes. Au contraire, I said, neither "they" nor their corporations do time, except on golfing junkets.

In the face of the horribollah of the Mideast, my plaint can sound like queer-quibbling, even to me. But rulings in New York, California, and many other states not only make gay people morally expendable, they also have very real life consequences, even in Massachusetts, the home of gay marriage.

On June 26, 2006, my good friend Eric Rofes died suddenly in Provincetown. Each day it becomes clearer what a huge loss his death is for the gay community. Eric, almost fifty-two, organizer, educator, historian, sex radical, feminist, thinker, and writer, had cut his activist teeth in Boston in the 1970s. He lived in San Francisco and was in his beloved Ptown for the summer working on his twelfth book.

His death was discovered on Monday night, and by Tuesday evening many of his friends from his old Boston Gay Mafia days, now national gay leaders, had gathered in Ptown. Crispin, Eric's partner of sixteen years, finally arrived from San Francisco late Tuesday afternoon, stunned and stricken. He had in hand Eric's power of attorney, his will, and their domestic-partner papers. We found the only cantor on Cape Cod through the yellow pages and planned Eric's funeral.

Crispin wanted an autopsy to learn the cause of death. Despite his and Eric's sixteen years together, he was told that he would need Eric's mother's authorization.

You do not want to anger gay lawyers who are heads of national

organizations in their time of grief. The autopsy was performed and revealed a massive heart attack and undiagnosed congestive heart failure, important information for Eric's surviving brother.

Crispin wanted to honor Eric's wishes for cremation and was informed again that he would need the mother's authorization. Again the angry gay lawyers on cell phones.

Eric had powerful, relentless, connected friends to fulfill his final wishes. But what of other Crispins, in small and large towns, paralyzed by grief, going it alone, with no energy or agency to decide what will become of their partner's remains? They are the collateral accidents from unjust impulses.

......................................................................................................

# Happy Returns

### January 2007

The night before the midterm elections, I left the United States with my gal pal on a business trip to Kenya. Hers, not mine. I was not sad to leave. Despite the late tide of very cautious optimism, my cynicism had me worried that at the last moment the American people would again fall, sheeplike, for some Rovian strategery. Gas prices went down at the voting booth. Abramoff was sent upriver. Saddam Hussein was sentenced the Sunday before the election! If Negroponte could have arranged it, Hussein would have been hanged on Monday. I worried that when I returned, everyone would be sipping Woolite cosmos.

We laid over in London, where the papers were speculating that Bush was on the sauce again. We finally landed twenty-four hours later in Nairobi—have I told you how much I love Ambien?—and got news that the Dems had taken the House! There was toyi-toying by the luggage carousel. Even the Kenyans were happy. They, of course, hope that their favorite son, Barack Obama, will be the next president of the United States, as if that will somehow solve their problems.

Before we could get more election news, we flew north to the Rift Valley, out of range and off the grid. On my birthday, someone managed to pick up an errant BlackBerry signal or perhaps a drumbeat and we heard that Rumsfeld had resigned. For my sixtieth I hope to get smoke signals that George is to appear before the International War Crimes Tribunal. Impeachment is too good for him.

Africa is so stunningly beautiful, you can see why those chilled old white Europeans just had to have it. The long-range effects of their colonizing—genocide, overpopulation, civil war, illiteracy, poverty, environmental havoc—foretell the dire long-range consequences of Boy George's colonizing binge, I mean democratizing campaign, in Iraq.

Each time in the last six years that we have traveled out of the United States we have dreaded the return. From Lula's new Brazil. From Mary Robinson and Mary Patricia McAleese's Ireland. This time was different. When we landed, everyone was a week ahead in their gloating, but I assure you, I have caught up. I had shows immediately, and selfishly worried that the electoral change would be a hard adjustment. Comedically, I admit to having grown lazy. What has been bad for us has been good for me. But no worries! Maybe no more goose-stepping yes-men parroting the Republican Party line. But kudos to the nutty, messy Democrats. Arguing behind closed doors, then spilling, brawling, into the streets. It's pluralism, baby!

Is it me or is there a slight uptick for women? Despite the grand mufti of Australia's pronouncement that a woman without a hijab is like a piece of raw meat, despite our exporting fundamentalism and all its misogynist works to Canada, I sense a slight winter solstice turn toward the light. I count the defeat of the antichoice measure in South Dakota, the many women elected and reelected, the likelihood of a woman, a socialist, as the next president of France. Hey, even Britney dumped Kevin.

So I will be smiling that night in January when that gnarly little guy swings open that big wooden door and barks, "Madame Speaker." And I will watch happily when Nancy Pelosi sits pertly upright in her double-knits. As she sits next to Dick "Waterboard" Cheney, I will wish they could insert thought bubbles over her head. Nancy, unblinking and poised, next to Dick, slumped and grumpy, will sit

behind George as he labors through his "If I Did It" State of the Union address. Somehow Speaker Pelosi will exercise restraint and not clock him one from behind with her gavel. No such restraint for me! I will not be drinking a Woolitini. I will be munching New York City's own trans-fat-less freedom fries.

........................................................................................................

# Stupor Bowl

### February 2007

Truth be told—and it so rarely is—I generally do the crossword puzzle while my gal pal is watching Sunday football. It is good for my brain, even if occasionally I have to Google my inadequacies because I am really not up on my lakes in Australia. *Google* is now a verb—I Google, you Google, she Googles, everyone Googles. It has ruined our fighting. We used to spend hours with friends at dinner, soddenly arguing about the date of Martina Navratilova's amazing physical transformation or the number of times she defeated Chris Evert.

"It had to be 1990. I had just broken up with Barb when she had that affair with Celia and I swear Martina's forearms got me through my homicidal moments. I still hate that Celia."

"No, it was 1991 or I'll drink another shot of tequila."

Not now.

Someone invariably gets out some annoying handheld device and Googles the answer. Now all we have left to argue about are feeeeeeeeeeeeeeelings. Ugh.

But the Super Bowl is different. I save the puzzle for the endless postgame analysis and to avoid my gal pal's inevitable slide into post-football funk.

For me, the national football holy day is all about the snacks and a chance to wear black Capri slacks around the house. And dance to Prince. Our company was a raucous gang of gals and one guy who left after the first play, and some snacks. As I was trundling platters back

and forth, I heard shrieks about the Bears quarterback: "How did he get this far? Why can't they get rid of him? Oh no! He fumbled it! What is he thinking? He's terrrrrrrrrrrrible." It reminded me of our screams during the State of the Union blather.

The game was boring, so I glanced at the *New York Times Magazine* between canapés. The world might be going to hell in a lovely handbasket, but the big story was about designer-dog fights. The article was intended to get folks fired up about the next big sporting event, the Westminster Dog Show at Madison Square Garden. Apparently people with way too much time on their hands are getting pugs to mount Yorkshires, begetting pugshires; beagles to mount bassets, begetting bagels; and Labradors to mount poodles, begetting Labradoodles. In the article, poodles come off like slutty species traitors. Dog purists are in high lather.

There was a touchdown and things were getting sort of interesting, so I quickly scanned to see if there was any mention of that anti-gay-marriage trope that same-sex marriage leads inevitably to man-on-dog sex. Pennsylvania's ex-senator Rick Sanctimoron loved to bring that one up. For him and many others, gay people are a thin firewall between men and their pets. The cross-species breeding was perhaps a sign of a dangerous breach. I quickly scanned for any references to gayshires, fagadoodles, or Cornish gay men. There is never any mention of woman-on-dog sex, but no lesbidoodles or dykedles were cited. I guess we will just have to wait for the cat show.

May I offer you some kibble?

.................................................................................

# Amazing Grace

## April 2007

In March of 1989, pre-full-blown March Marketing Madness, I was traveling through the old Denver airport and—surprise, surprise—was delayed by a weather event of some sort and had hours to kill. I

had been hoping to get home in time to watch the women's NCAA basketball finals with some raucous friends. It did not look good.

After I resigned myself to a long delay, I found a smoky airport bar, ordered a beverage, and thus felt entitled to ask the bartender if he would turn one of the many TVs to the women's final game. The what? The women's basketball finals. You sure it's on? After much cajoling, he finally sighed and, all put out, reached up and changed the channel. Although it was a Tennessee rout of Louisiana Tech, it was a pleasure to watch the women athletes.

It was not a pleasure to have to sit and listen to the men and some women in the bar wonder why that game was on instead of hockey, who those Amazons were, and other pre-Imus idiocies. I glared at any complainer, dared the bartender to touch the dial, and marvel to this day that I did not get into a barroom brawl. I was ready.

On this thirty-fifth anniversary of Title IX, an equal-opportunity measure that still must be defended from Bush late-night signing statement shenanigans, the women's final was another Tennessee win, this time over the scrappy Rutgers team coached by the eloquent, inspirational C. Vivian Stringer. We in the Northeast, suffering through the insufferable Knicks and Nets season, were cheered by the improbable success of our local Rutgers varsity team with all their talented freshman athletes.

As the Scarlet Knights were settling back into midterms and dreams of next year, Don Imus launched the word bombs you have heard a million times and all hell broke loose. For anyone who has chanced on the doubly formatted *Imus in the Morning* show, this was not new behavior. The *I White Man* show has for years been a clubby, chummy safe place where mostly men correspondents, politicos, and celebrities could josh and mix it up with the curmudgeon in the cowboy hat.

Perhaps it was the Obama effect, or the sixtieth anniversary of Jackie Robinson's breaking the color line in baseball, that tipped Imus's behavior into the last-straw category, but enough was finally enough. The 24/7 drama has been about sexism, racism, free speech, the market, etc. You have heard it all. I trust Pat Summitt has sent a note.

I head off to Pennsylvania this weekend to watch my niece, a freshman on the Gettysburg College women's varsity lacrosse team, a

strong contender to win their Division Three and go on to the finals. Her name is Grace. She is fierce, fast, has great hands. I will be the fan in the stands whooping inordinately with all the pent-up fire I did not get to vent in that Denver airport bar. It will be for Grace and her team, of course, but it will also be for the double unformatting of the *I White Man* and all that it means. I am so ready.

## B Is for Benchmark

### July 2007

Apiculturalists have answered that famous Hamlet multiple-choice, existential question: (a) to be or (b) not to be. The answer is (b), not to be. On the West Coast, 60 percent of their bee colonies have gone missing. On the overachieving East Coast, 70 percent are has bee-ns. This latest plague upon the land is called colony collapse disorder (CCD).

CCD occurs when a hive's inhabitants suddenly disappear, leaving only queens, eggs, and a few immature workers. Sounds like a planning meeting I once attended for a gay protest at the annual White House Easter Egg Roll. Each day I check urban legend debunking sites for news that some bored high schoolers from North Dakota started the rumor. So far nothing.

Apian scientists posit many causes for the deaths of the bees: mites, pesticides, radioactive waves, cell phones, genetically altered foods, global warming, or all of the above. I think it is Starbucks in the groundwater. Absorbed by plants, the caffeine makes the bees busy-busy, then crazy-busy, then dead from overwork. No more little bees' knees jutting from peonies, obscenely pantalooned in pollen.

Albert Einstein, one Alberto we can believe, said that after the bees disappear, humanity has about four years left. I do not want to sound like some Nostra Dame, but we have already begun to see a

corollary collapse. It is BBCC, baby-boomer colony collapse. Quite frankly, I could not be happier. And I am one.

My baby-boom generation has been endlessly, tediously fascinating to itself. Spawn of World War II, we grew up on Spock. We rocked from Elvis to the Beatles. The Vietnam War was our first quagmire. We did drugs, inhaled, fought for civil rights for women, blacks, and gays. Love meant never having to say you're sorry. Our idealism was supposedly killed with Martin Luther King and the Kennedys.

Some late boomers got conservative, corporate, rich, did cocaine. In our inevitable fifties, many did Viagra, Botox, and hormones. Aided by our Uncle Toms—Brokaw and Hanks—the rich, who had not served in the first quagmire because they had other priorities, grew nostalgic for those so-called greatest generation wars. When attacked in 2001, we were pumped up and ready. We gave ourselves rhetorical goose bumps about freedom goose-stepping. Iraqnam.

Talkin' 'bout my generation, George Bush, king baby boomer in chief, and his loyal cronies have not represented well. The defining moment of his "administration" is not 9/11 but *Reno 911,* a cable cop show whose tagline is "No one does a better job of not doing a better job." The BushClintonBushClinton (BCBC) double helix of hubris is the buzzkill of BBCC. Though Hillary is a woman, there is cold comfort on the farm with "You go to the polls with the candidate you have, not the one you wish you had."

Now in our sixties, we are terrorized by death, and of course no one has ever experienced that quite so exquisitely. It is unseemly for us to be called baby boomers. We are geezer boomers. We should just get out of the way—work for Habitat for Humanity, do Meals on Wheels, be literacy volunteers. I am sorry. Our work here is done. It is time to step away from the hive.

..................................................................................................

# TGI 9/12

### September 2007

Thank God it's 9/12. This morning we commemorate that morning six years ago when we all woke up, if we had slept, or slept fitfully, and for a waking breath everything was the same. Coffee, paper, jump in the shower. Then—say it isn't so—it hit. Despite groggy hope, we remembered what had happened the day before, 9/11/2001, our national Alive Day.

Nine-eleven is now a very real quatrosyllabic number, a fulcrum of before and after, that second when the tide does shift. The day was excruciating this year, the new longest day of the year. The day was tropically muggy, and on TV all day the military junta was laying out the fantasy league so-called surge. A dirge.

In other years, before the anniversary of 9/11, I had prepared, steeled myself to the sadness, made plans to be with a neighbor whose firefighter husband had been killed. This time, like soldiers in Iraq, I was unarmored; I had let my guard down. By two p.m. I was restless and sad, claustrophobic in our apartment across the hall from new neighbors. I could not read one more tediously brilliant article about how bad it is. The war, the subprime mortgage rolling disaster, the trifecta of hypocrisy—Foley, Vitter, Craig.

That was when I remembered a small notice in the Sunday paper of a memorial service for Molly Ivins, at the Ethical Culture Society Hall, scheduled for four p.m. on, of course, 9/11.

Never have I been happier to go to a memorial service. The soggy, sad crowd slogged in while a montage of photos of Molly—a long-legged sailor; smiling aunt hoisting a gleeful niece; wide-mouth, head-back laugher; placard-carrying, hell-raising protester; wheelchair-bound, bald, and mugging in a Fox News cap, receiving an award—looped on a screen onstage.

Calvin Trillin, Maya Angelou, John Leonard, Gail Collins, Kath-

leen Chalfant, and Lou Dubose spoke of Molly as friend, writer, editor, storyteller, river rafter, partier, bawdy Texas babe, and activist. They all quoted her hilarious lines. It was she who, Cassandra-like, in the *Texas Observer* had warned of being bushwhacked by the Shrub from Texas. She wanted to live to see George Bush out of office, but she died from the breast cancer she had lived with for years.

There are memorials and there are memorials. As I shuffled out into the quagmire of New York, I felt reenergized by the buoyant life of Molly Ivins, my co-columnist at the *Progressive* magazine for twelve years. She practiced the power of political satire and activism. Thank goodness for Molly Ivins.

....................................................................................

# Rudimentary
### November 2007

You do not want to play Scrabble with Annie Dillard. Not that she'd invite you over. But if she did, after offering you an excellent adult beverage and perhaps leaving a Lark smoldering in a tartan plaid beanbag ashtray, she would kick your ass. She knows lots of words, and she knows exactly where and when to put them down. Every one racks up at least a double word score. As a Scrabble buff and a nineteen-year off-and-on resident of Provincetown, the setting for Dillard's new novel, *The Maytrees*, I have walked the dunes and I know the scenes, like this one, that she describes:

> *Above the Atlantic's rim she saw a rain's fallstreaks curve. A stillness of empty space marked all she saw. It was this loping shore of mineral silence people meant when they said "the dunes." The surface of the moon might look like this: rudimentary.*

Dillard captures Ptown in all its seasons, summer people, and constant tidal changes. *The Maytrees* fills the fiction gap between

Provincetown memoirs such as Mary Heaton Vorse's *Time and the Town* and Mark Doty's *Heaven's Coast* and Karen Krahulik's historical study *Provincetown: From Pilgrim Landing to Gay Resort.*

Dillard claims that after writing *The Maytrees* she is tired, and she is not going to write any more novels. This is understandable, but it is a loss. An eight-year project, *The Maytrees* was originally 1,200 pages long and packed with historical and natural detail, but Dillard decided that her simple love story could not support all that. Although she fully renders the characters of the Cape and the Cape itself as a character, in the 217 pages that remain, one wishes the edited material could be an addendum to the book, like the extra features on a DVD.

Set in the 1940s, *The Maytrees* is the love story of Lou Bigelow and Toby Maytree. They court, marry, and have a son, Petie. Toby leaves Lou for the town hoyden, Deary Hightoe, and the two move to Maine. Lou raises Petie and achieves a life without resentment. Twenty years later, Deary develops heart problems, and Toby returns with her to Provincetown. Lou cares for Deary, who is, after all, her old friend, and Lou and Toby reconcile. These are the bare bones of the story.

Today, the few remaining old-time year-rounders often refer to Ptown as the world's largest open-air insane asylum. *The Maytrees* is peopled with a supporting cast of nonconforming characters: Reevadare Weaver, the much-married, much-hennaed, BYO-everything party giver; Cornelius Blue, a full-bearded denizen of the dune shacks, the remote, falling-down artists' dwellings along the ocean; Hiram and Elaine Cairo, professors from New York; Jane, their non-dissertation-writing daughter, who marries Cornelius, twenty years her senior; and Lou, Toby, and Deary themselves. Deary is an architect who sleeps in the dunes wrapped in sails because "she claimed to like the way the starlight smelled on the sand." Toby, a veteran of World War II, moves houses in Ptown for a living and writes epic poems in red composition books.

Toby leaves Lou the day after Petie is hurt in a bicycle accident. Toby uses his wife's willingness to forgive the driver who hit her son to bolster his decision, although he himself will ultimately benefit from Lou's capacity for forgiveness. Lou, who had watched her mother polish her grudge against her father, who abandoned the family, as "the sole project for the balance of her life," decides that she will not be " 'Poor Mom' with periodic walk-on roles as grieving and piteous vic-

tim." After her dune neighbor, Cornelius, says, "Lou, I wish you'd stop poisoning yourself," she hikes up the Pilgrim Monument, a granite tower in the center of town:

> *From the top she looked at flat sky, flat sea and flat land. She was ready to want to stop this. Thereby she admitted—barely—that she could choose to stop. For one minute by her watch, she imagined she liked Maytree impartially. For only one minute by her watch she saw him for himself. That day, having let go one degree of arc only, for one minute, she sighted relief. Here was something she could do. She could climb the monument every day and work on herself as a task. She had nothing else to do. Their years together were good. He was already gone. All she had to do for peace was let him go.*

Her monumental, quotidian grieving frees her, and thus free, she hopes "scandalously" to live her own life. She tries to hear her own thoughts. She reclaims "what she had forfeited of her own mind, if any. She took pains to keep outside the word acceleration." Her dune shack becomes the room of her own. "The bay and ocean and daytime sky did not change. Lou lived in color fields. By habit, she ignored the Cape's manmade changes." She paints again. A true New Englander, she cuts out all radio but the Red Sox. She learns to look out for "resentment, self-cherishing and envy. Though town, national and world life gave her fits, she formed the habit of deflecting them before they dug in."

Freed from the "tar pit" of grief and the miasma of town gossip, she wonders, "Why take personal offense if two fall in love?" She enjoys the newsy letters Cornelius receives from Maytree, orders his new book of poetry, and writes to Maytree and Deary, inviting them to come back to Provincetown.

As the real estate boom and big money—for some, at least—have hit Ptown with a plague of gussied-up, airtight houses equipped with motion-sensor security lights, I read with nostalgia of the Ptown of old. Dillard says she wanted to call her book *Romantic Comedy about Light Pollution,* but her publishers did not like her joke.

As a manual for transcending life's sorrow and savoring life's joys, *The Maytrees* is the most practical of self-help books.

# Our State of Affairs
# Is a Great State Fair

### January 2008

Though I was born in Buffalo, when I was ten we moved to Syracuse, "the home of the New York State Fair!" my mother chirped excitedly like some central New York booster on speed. I already hated summer fairs, having been dragged through the baby goat barn at the Erie County Fair. I always dreaded summer's end, not because school was about to start up and I had not lost ten pounds, but because the state fair was about to begin.

That meant being unable to beg off attending by claiming that I was perfecting my jackknife at the city pool. On the hottest day we would sit stuck in traffic, bare backs of legs stuck to the leatherette of our Ford Fairlane; park in an open scrub field, knowing that we would never see our car again unless we waited until everyone had left; and slog with other family pods to the long lines at the arching gates into a shadeless hell.

The fairgrounds were located next to the Bristol-Myers plant and Crucible Steel mill that everyone knew was dumping into Onondaga Lake. The annual spring regatta generally had the slowest times because no life-respecting coxswain wanted to win and get tossed into the lake. Supposedly the site has been eco-vacuumed to make room for the Carousel Mall, but friends say that if you toss a cigarette butt in the parking lot, the macadam will ignite. "Third eye" takes on new meaning. That vision has prompted some local developers to expand and build Destiny, a mall bigger than the Pentagon-shaped one in Minnesota.

On humid, hot fair days the yellowish chemical air carried fried-dough particulate matter from the midway. The festival of junk food mocked the goody-two-shoes home ec pavilion. Even at ten I pitied

performers, squinting and sweating on the main stage. Loser! Your career is over! Because of early gyroscopic inner-ear damage from spinning/falling-down contests with my brothers, I hate rides. If you ever see a picture of me, hair blown back, in mid-Munch *Scream*, elbows locked, it will be me on the stationary horse on the carousel. I loved the hostility of bumper cars, but that was just me blowing off steam.

All this to perhaps explain why I loathe Iowa. The Gateway to the Rectangular States. Not even three million people. All of them farmers who have nothing better to do than pout if a candidate does not have a meal at their house, wear their "I Heart Huckabee" button, and pretend to be undecided so they can get face time on camera and caucus endlessly.

Once a friend interrupted me mid-whine with her theory about why the primaries start in Iowa. She said, "Think about it: All that open space. All those abandoned barns. I think they are making crystal meth and all the campaign reporters load up there to get through the campaign." It certainly explains Chris Matthews.

Iowans do not have to farm at all. The farm-subsidy pyramid scam actually pays them not to plant. They feel terrible about it. Then when they are done deciding the fate of the nation, the Children of the Corn State put on their mesh caps, hop in their giant mobile homes, gas up at three bucks a gallon, and head on down to some trailer parks for a few months on the Gulf. Jaw with their friends in the Iowa enclave about the sorry state of the world.

Hey, they make up stories about Manhattanites all the time. They hiss we are a Sssssssssanctuary City. We are Sodom and Gomorrah. Oh, and the hotel room rates are too high. I resent America's being held hostage to Iowa. I hate the roller-coaster ride of campaigns, especially because it starts in Iowa. Where are those bumper cars when I need them?

# Curb Your Cynicism

## February 2008

My partner and I go to our local elementary school to vote in the primary. The school is justly beloved for its dynamic principal, innovative curriculum, parental involvement, and special needs program. With all manner of wheelchairs and walking devices, the first floor looks like a good day at Lourdes. It is a victim of its success, and so overcrowded it has had to move many special programs out of the school.

We walk past the PTA moms hawking baked goods for the school. "The croissants are low-fat." We give them a ten but do not take anything. They are chirpingly grateful.

We walk into a steamy, Diane Arbus, low-ceilinged inner room smelling faintly of green sawdust and cooked cabbage. I suspect that since it is early, the election officials are still just getting their system down. We are the fourth and fifth voters from our district.

The older woman I am directed to does not hear or see that well and seems flummoxed with the multitasking of finding Clinton on her list—"Can you spell it?"—and assigning me a number. Five. The big lever to open the voting booth curtain is jammed. I cast my vote for someone who will have to deal with global warming, gay issues, education, aging issues, the economy, voting reform. And that war.

We vote, walk out, and breathe deeply. We walk by a young woman by the playground fence, at the mandatory distance from the polling place, surreptitiously murmuring "Hillary" and passing out homemade fliers like they were nickel bags. A woman with a regulation Obama placard stands in silent vigil across the street.

This Super Tuesday, it is Carnival in other parts of the world. In the United States, it is the national semifinals of *American Idol* and there is a late surge by a talented young man who can kick out a speech like nobody's business. The handsome Mormon business guy

is lip-syncing Ronald Reagan. The white-haired vet is cracking straight jokes. No matter the talents of the woman contestant, she is to be judged by *Survivor* rules.

Tomorrow is Ash Wednesday. I am going to daub a big bindi of ash on my furrowed brow and try to give up cynicism for Lent.

······························································································

# Late Adopters
## March 2008

Finally! A phrase to describe me. Not just "tired old white woman for Hillary." I am what is called "a late adopter."

This is not to be confused with some of my older lesbian friends, who pull me aside and whisper, "Barb and I are thinking of adopting."

"A child?!"

"Well, what else?"

"No offense, but when you're sixty-five, your kid will be fifteen."

"And your point is?"

"You remember when you were fifteen?"

"Not really."

"You know, they have Zipcars now. You just use them for a few hours and then return them with a quarter tank of gas."

"Again, your point?"

"Why not just try a Zipkid, a six-month-old baby. Try a colicky one, then a thirteen-year-old. See how it goes."

"There's no such thing as Zipkids."

Their loss.

I have found that when friends are on the Magical Mystery Tour of Must Have Children, there is no reasoning with them. They seem to contemplate only the process of getting and having the child, not the screaming late-night fights about homework or appropriate footwear for winter. I thought Zipkids would be a bracing slap out of it, but

my let-me-step-on-your-smile insurance friends say the liability and bonding would be too expensive.

No, the purview of my late adopting is technology. Though I have come out as a lesbian and as a Hillary supporter, I have a very difficult time coming out as someone who does not bank online. I had a lot of shame, until banks started disappearing and I felt positively prescient. Turns out when banks compete, we lose. For me, using the Forever Stamp is daringly technological.

According to consultants who study such things, the causes of late adoption of technology are fear of time-consuming upgrades, satisfaction with one's current technology, and inertia. I have neither internal nor external drive toward more megamemory. When that annoying prompt about available updates appears, I always opt for "remind me later." I have not yet gotten back to the eight-track people. I am a thorough laggard.

My girlfriend is an early, eager adopter and proselytizer. She always tells me what I need. She reads the technology section of the paper. One morning without prompting, she read me the specs on the new lightweight Apple AirBook—thin, no internal drive, and not much memory. I was absorbed in boldfaced gossip and half thought she was describing me. I was hurt. She got one of the first iPhones. She got two. She gave me one. I put it in the closet. She upgrades hers all the time. The icons on my iPhone still do not wiggle.

Only recently have I stopped thinking of a computer as a typewriter with a TV screen and stopped resenting the printer as a second entity in another room. Truthfully, the times that I have upgraded to a new computer have been less about needing more memory or more speed, or getting my girlfriend off my case and more about hygiene. The keyboard was filthy.

Because of some mild untreated OCD thing, my girlfriend is totally shkeeved about nail clipping. She cannot bear the sound of it and fears the dangerous killing shards of nails sent flying through the air, embedding into random corneas passing by. Emery boarding is torture for her. Oddly, her own clipping and abrading does not faze her.

She will not let me trim my nails at the bathroom sink. She will not allow it in the den, even after the room has been put under a *Dexter*-like plastic wrapping. Nowhere on the Upper West Side. Certain parts of rural Iowa are okay. I would have long, curlicued, freak-

show, ribbed, yellowing fingernails if it were not for the fact that I travel. It is actually why I travel.

Though sometimes when I am sure she is safely at work and I am at my desk, I do take a swipe at an annoying hangnail or raggedy fingernail. First I put on my safety glasses. What magnetic force field causes that fingernail-sized piece of shrapnel to fly, like a heat-seeking laser-guided missile, to the computer on my desk? Though the half cup of coffee still has some heat, it never takes a hit. The shard lands and seeks shelter in the rabbit hole under the key of G. Or it hangs, partially exposed, on the lip of the Mac- precipice under the 7& key, until I try to retrieve it with a moistened fingertip and clumsily push it into the keyboard abyss.

I am sure there are computer detailers who would take the thing apart and give it a good vacuum. But I am too embarrassed to take it to such a place. I know I could just drop it off. But I would have to go back and endure their looks. They would be trying to check out my nails.

When I do get a new computer, it must come with a Zip I.T. kid.

# Fighting Weight
## April 2008

On election night in 2000, a night that lasted a month, we had a small dinner party to watch the Bush vs. Gore election returns. It was a simpler time then, children. Through the night, the state of Florida changed colors like a crazy traffic light: red, blue, then yellow.

Some guests stopped eating, forkfuls frozen inches away from open mouths. Who could chew with such dropped jaws? One guest was gnawing absentmindedly on the rickrack on a couch pillow. I could have served Kibbles 'n Bits. Other guests decided to drink their dinner instead. When they staggered out, Florida was hanging off the United States like a sad, cautionary, bunchless banana.

That was the night I started to eat everything in sight and to root out things I had hidden from myself for years. I ignored the "best used by 1998" warnings on Oreos. I became reacquainted with butter and butter delivery systems like lobster and popcorn. I ate Cheetos again, whole grab bags of them. The yellow residue on my fingers was a shade off Florida.

On December 12, 2000, the Supreme Court essentially voted to select George W. Bush as president for the sake of the union. Big mistake for the union. On January 20, 2001, Bush was sworn in as the forty-third president of the United States. I had been eating nervously and nonstop for more than two months.

After a photo retoucher had done all he could on promo pictures on my sixth CD, short of zeliging in Angelina Jolie's body, I decided it was up to me to get the lines out from under my chin. A week after the inauguration, I attended my first meeting of Weight Watchers. I felt like my weight was the only thing I could control.

The new Weight Watchers system is not like the WW of old, with the daunting science-project food scales, calculators, and smoking beakers. It is based on a system of points determined by a ratio of calories, fat, and fiber with time-off bonus points for the good behavior of regular exercise. A handy slide rule does all the figuring. It is so easy even I could use it.

The WW point system is not to be confused with the immigration point system later proposed by Attorney General (accent on the general) Alberto Gonzales. No slide rule invented could do the algorithms of incoming education and earning capability divided by skin tone and terror potential, so the plan was dropped. I am just glad I am already here. By my rough calculus, I am about 117 points short of entry. Good thing Native Americans did not have a point system. There would have been a lot of disappointed Puritans.

My regular WW meeting was a block off the Columbia University campus. To get to the meeting, I would walk resentfully through throngs of slinky college kids, still possessed of high metabolisms, who could and were eating and drinking anything they wanted.

In the basement of an old Presbyterian church I was one of the few white people. Another was a spindly wise old Jewish woman. She was a regular, with a smoky, gravelly voice. She would occasionally pipe up with advice. On the topic of the dangers of coleslaw, her on-

point pearl was "You know you can rinse the coleslaw." I said, "But that would just be cabbage." She said smugly, "Exactly."

The group leader had lost fifty-three pounds and had Kept It Off for Eight Years. He was crazy about the new WW. He was also a giant, flaming queen. No one seemed to care.

He gave simple, nearly primal advice. Do not eat anything bigger than your hand. The first knuckle of your index finger equals a tablespoon. Do not go to the all-you-can-eat buffet with your plate. Scout it out first and decide what you want. Go back with your plate. Put the food on your plate but do not let any of the foods on your plate touch. And do not go back. Do not eat white food. Eat dark green vegetables. Drink water.

He was cheeky and relentlessly positive with life messages. He was no snarky, punitive, skinny bitch. On Valentine's Day, the traditional When Chocolate Is Love Festival, he reframed the message from romance to a passion for life. Then he rolled a dinged-up, out-of-tune upright piano into the middle of the room and banged out "You've Got to Have Heart," like the Champagne Lady on *The Lawrence Welk Show* but without the underarm flab, while a fleshy, mortified preteen sullenly turned huge flip pages so we all could sing along. That week I lost another two pounds.

In six months, as George Bush settled into his new digs, mistook his luck for a mandate, appointed cryogenic throwbacks from the Ford years, thought about stem cells, not terror cells, and stroked his preemptiveness, I lost fifty pounds. My WW steely self-control was polar opposite to the complete lack of political control I felt with W. I wish Al Gore could have been in my group. Nine-eleven, the lead-up to the war in Afghanistan, the shredding of the Constitution, the invasion of Iraq, Guantánamo, Abu Ghraib, Terri Schiavo, Supreme Court—all former invitations to life's food court—did not tempt me. I would not give him that satisfaction.

Of course, I worry that when my enabler in chief, with his bite-sized midges of empty rhetoric, leaves office, there might be some recidivism. But the fat-cat years of Bush have taught me to be vigilant, alert, totally conscious of my intake. Thanks to him, it is not a diet; it is a way of life.

# Sisterhood of the Traveling Pantsuit

Sometimes during the Democratic primary season, when I would return from a three-day road trip of my own, incoherent, immobilized from the fatigue of performing, being on, fighting jet lag, doing interviews, running my small business, I would flash on my sister-in-law Hillary Clinton in her tenth month of 24/7 travel days and wonder, "How does she do it?" Of course she had her own hair, makeup, and wardrobe people, her own plane and a travel office, but still. Others wondered, "How dare she do it?" What she had the nerve to call a campaign, after the Iowa primaries others called a death watch. She made some wrong decisions—believing in her own inevitability, keeping her campaign manager too long, running an air war, not a ground war, and not fist-bumping Bill into tomorrow. But I am glad she did it. While some wrote her obitchuary, she wrote a page of history.

# Why Not Hillary?

**March 2005**

Okay, I did not leave on the four-year gay cruise that sailed down the Potomac on January 21, nor am I planning to leave the country. I already live in the tiny island nation of New York City. But the state of Washington looks mighty tempting. The actual state, not whatever sorry state of the union George read to us about.

Washington State's governor and both senators are women. The prominence of women is attributed to several factors: Early women pioneers engendered abiding respect for women's contribution; outrage over the Clarence Thomas confirmation hearings caused women to seek and win political office; the state's weak party structures do not foster strong old-boys networks; the high-tech entrepreneurial culture created businesswomen who write political checks. No one has mentioned record levels of caffeine consumption, but my research people are looking into it. In addition to the trifecta at the top, 44 percent of Washington's Supreme Court justices and 33 percent of its state legislators are women.

And I know, according to Lawrence Summers, I am way over my head here even dealing with percentages. Lordy, lordy, where are my smelling salts? Nationally, 50 percent of bachelor's degrees in math and science are earned by women, who make up only 10 percent of college faculties in those subjects. I am woozy! In his speech to an academic conference, the president of Harvard offered that women may be innately unsuited for math and science. Summers suggested that one of the main obstacles to their tenure tracks was their biological clocks. I am as outraged as the next sister, but you can be sure I will be using the "Suddenly Last Summers" rationale as an excuse if I ever get an IRS audit.

It is still mind-boggling to me that we have not yet had a woman president or vice president. That darned Aspermative Action. In Fin-

land or maybe it is Sweden (and I am a little geographically challenged, but hey, I am not the president), they have had a woman president for five years. Long enough to cause such a shift in the paradigm that one young boy asked her, "Can a man be president?"

As the White House Project has been asking for ten years, "Why not a woman?" According to the WHP, women leaders bubble up from other positions of power. Women are woefully underrepresented in those positions: 14 percent of the Senate, 14 percent of the House, 18 percent of governorships. Those numbers make me swoon too.

Oprah does not seem interested in buying the presidency, so why not Hillary? As a gay friend of mine said, "She's the only Democrat with the balls to run and win."

She is a great campaigner. When she ran for senator, against Rick Lazio, I was visiting my family in Syracuse. I was dismayed to see all those upstate lawns pinioned with Lazio signs, but Hillary ran a listening tour and I swear she shook hands or shared a food product with every single upstate voter.

My only hesitation, other than that I do not like a lot of her politics, is that she will reactivate all those rabid Hillary haters. But online I found that Haters of Hillary really have never stopped. HOHs are still talking about the Bride of Clintonstein. That Hillary will run as a moderate to win and then do whatever she pleases! That a Hillary presidency would be a dynastic horror show! That she is a pretender to the throne! That her history is "littered with mysterious deaths, immoral behavior, and shady financial dealings." In short, she has what it takes to be president.

I just wish she would not run in 2008. Women are always given the most impossible cleanup jobs. And Jeb ("Meet This Focker") Bush, sent on a tsunami tour to raise his profile, may be next in line. He can have the mess.

Hillary in 2012.

......................................................................................................

# "If you go down to the woods today . . ."

## July 2007

Let's review: If it's three, let it be. I just had to pull up a few sprouting milkweeds by the side of the house, didn't I? Gloveless, of course. It is not a rip-roaring case of poison ivy. It is more slow-moving, popping up along the veins of my right hand as if it is on a lazy summer rafting trip. Who knew I rested my face on my hand so much? I am working the Caladryl, getting everyone's trusted remedies, and bandaging where appropriate. Comparatively, I have a lovely first-world problem.

If, however, those three are one, as in triune, as in God, well, I cannot let that be. God's prod, the Widow Ratzinger, that old Prada-wearing Devil, cannot let it be either. He is bringing back the Latin mass. And not a moment too soon. No more hootenanny masses with guitars strumming "Let It Be." I for one could not be happier. Catholics are terrible singers. They are the only people I know who can sing and breathe in at the same time. And when they inhale in English, it sounds worse than when it is in Latin.

Pope Ed "Good Driver" Rimer also issued the top ten commandments of driving: Thou shalt not use thy cell phone whilst driving. Thou shalt not flip thy bird. Thou shalt not make assumptions about a fellow driver's mother's genetic lineage. At least I think that is what they said. Again the Latin. What's next? Bringing back S&M martyr worship and second-degree relic fetishizing? I personally am looking forward to buying a couple of indulgences. Although I guess I could just buy some carbon offsetting points and go right to heaven.

It's Bear Week here in Ptown! They are lots of fun, hairier, larger, and way less tweaked than the circuit party boys. The only downside of the week is that it is hell on the drains. Upside: Their pool parties are a blast. They run water down a turquoise waterslide, send salmon

up the slide, and the bears bat them away. I hope this year they will make me an honorary she-bear. Remember, do not keep any food-stuffs in your tent.

Speaking of she-bears, I have decided to throw my support to Hillary Clinton. I actually notified the LGBT for Hillary people and was told that I needed to get security clearance, and I have not heard anything back. It is taking so long, I am a little worried. The problem is that there is way too much tape on me in the public record. I cannot just refuse to turn over information. Who do you think I am? Dick Cheney?

I am just the kind of support Hillary needs. I support her despite the flak I am taking for it at home and at dinner parties. I support her despite her despites. That she voted for the war. That she took three days to clearly rebut Peter "homosexuality is immoral" Pace. That she is mush-mouthed on gay marriage. That it will once again be a woman's job to do cleanup after the boys.

Perhaps her people have heard that so far I only have seven "Top Ten Reasons I Support Hillary Clinton." She has the most experience. Yes, she is a hawk, but she is our hawk. And she comes with a pale male. She will cause Bill O'Really and Maureen Dowd's heads to blow up. Only women bleed. At this point I would rather be screwed over by a woman.

If I do not get clearance, I will be the head of the distaff She-Bears for Hillary 2008. We will have great pool parties. I will let you know when it is safe to shake my paw.

........................................................................................

# Hillaphobic Blowback

### November 2007

Coming out for Hillary Clinton in one-on-one or small group situations still reminds me of coming out as a lesbian. I am the lesbian, not Hillary, contrary to the sledgehammer innuendos of Ann Coulter.

Though we wish the best for everyone, Hillary may not be a lesbian. And that's okay.

And is it just me, or does Ann look a lot like the young, recumbent, and recently unwrapped King Tut?

Approaching the declaration for Hillary is like approaching that triple-salchow moment in a skating routine. Have I got the strength, the torque, the momentum, the sequins to come out to this person? Since I do not want my inner Dick Button murmuring disappointedly, "Aw, she only did a double," I declare my orientation for Hillary and prepare myself for the inevitable Hillaphobic blowback.

The other night at my study group dinner, it happened again. About eight of us meet monthly to discuss some dense progressive policy book we all claim to have read. I am generally seated at the kids' table. Before we got into the book discussion, we were doing our usual recap of recent political events. Several members always end up moaning and thudding their foreheads on the table in the "dovening-for-democracy" portion of the evening.

When we got to discussing the presidential campaign, my dear partner asked everyone to go around the table and announce who they were for and cruelly looked at me to start. I took what I knew would be my last bite of mushroom risotto for the evening and declared I was for Hillary.

A fine expectorated Chianti mist was settling from my friend's mouth as she bleated in horror, "Why?"

"Other than the fact that I think she would make Bill O'Really's head blow up and that she is the most qualified for the job —" I started.

"WHAT has she done?" my apoplectic friend screamed.

I continued, "I support her just so that I can get into fights with people about the appalling levels of sexism in the world," and daubed a small bit of mushroom off my neighbor's cuff.

Full disclosure: at the gym I have been listening to the audiotape of Susan Faludi's *The Terror Dream* on my iPod. Faludi reports so extensively and bloodlessly on the uses of 9/11 to restore "traditional" manhood, marriage, and maternity that she has gotten hysterical, vicious reviews that prove her point exactly. The men at the gym seem genuinely unsettled by my mirrored glowering at them.

It was as if I were one of those Dixie Chicks of Bridge and had held

up a handmade sign at an awards ceremony. Talk about gender card. I started to lay them out on the table. In South Carolina, a woman, perhaps Ann Coulter's grandmother, called Hillary a bitch, and John McCain did not cut her off. He has, no doubt, heard or even said worse. Maureen Dowd never met a woman she liked, making her a worthy *New York Times* columnist. Katie Couric cannot catch a break.

My friend rebutted from east, west, north, and south. Perhaps I overtricked when I endplayed her with "Why do you hate yourself so much?" I am not proud of it. Let the conversation continue.

.......................................................................

# Hillary's My Guy

## December 2007

No matter what you think of Hillary Clinton, her presidential campaign has restarted our national conversation about gender. And girl, do we ever need to keep talking. The last time we had a chat about it was in 1993, the so-called Year of the Woman. The conversation started in late June, so it was not even a full year, and most of the time was spent guessing the identity of the woman. In 2007 I try to do my part to keep the conversation from being reduced to little more than a dismissive crack about "playing the gender card."

Gender was at the heart of all kinds of seemingly unrelated events. Madame Speaker Nancy Pelosi was maligned for not reaching political benchmarks—the implication being that she fell short because she is a woman. But I like to point out that doing things constitutionally in the bright light of day takes longer than doing them unconstitutionally in the dark of night. I wish Pelosi had thought bubbles over her head during January's State of the Union (aka the "If I Did It") address.

When Don Imus referred to the Rutgers women's basketball team as "nappy-headed ho's" and "Amazons," it was not a proud moment

for people holding the white race cards. But the women's real offense was that they were playing like boys. Actually, better.

The Imus mess did give us a chance to read about women in sports, or at least near sports. Perhaps because the *New York Times* is a cost-cutting inch and a half narrower, and New York sports teams are so good (not), the sports section is unable to cover more—or any—women's sports. It is not limited to sports. If you were to read the obits every morning to your girlfriend, as I do, you would be able to announce after a quick scan, "Great news, honey, absolutely no women died today."

In other women's sort-of-sport news, the New York Knicks coach, Isiah Thomas—spiritual son of Justice Clarence Uncle Thomas, who is still ripped and resentful from back in 1991 about Anita Hill—maintained his petulance after the elegant Anucha Browne Sanders won her sexual harassment case against Thomas and Madison Square Garden. Sprinter Marion Jones also proved she was a class act as she apologized for her juice use.

In television, suits are still confining talent by gender, whether or not they admit it. When Katie Couric was allowed to break the testosterone ceiling and sit solo as nightly news reader, primetime news was of course past its prime. Still, her impudence was noted by Mr. Bitter, Dan Rather. Rosie O'Donnell, fresh from being fresh on *The View*, was unable to make a deal to do late-night comedy. Ellen DeGeneres, who seems less comfortable with the lesbian card she was dealt than her straight guests do, was allowed humanity by playing the canine card.

Can a woman handle the presidency? Oh, come on. But America is pretty much the last of the Western nations to get it. Our big democratic United States seems even more preposterous with its sexist doubts now that Ireland, New Zealand, Finland, Switzerland, the Philippines, Liberia, Germany, Norway, Chile, and Argentina have elected women heads of state. And do not forget the queens! In England, Denmark, the Netherlands, and the Village.

In the Middle East, gender is still a conversation nobody wants to have. After our friend and ally Saudi Arabia sentenced a nineteen-year-old woman, gang-raped fourteen times, to ninety lashes for violating Saudi segregation laws forbidding men and women from as-

sociating, I waited for our international image ambassador, Mr. Karen Hughes, to say something. Naturally, Hughes did nada. On appeal, the Saudi woman's punishment was increased to two hundred lashes and six months in prison for trying to influence the judiciary through the media. Somebody get her Paris Hilton's number.

Here is something worth talking about: Gender multiplied in 2007. At least that is how it seems to Middle America. A lot of us knew it all along. When the transgender card is played and the T is dropped from LGBT in an amended Employment Non-Discrimination Act, I like to point out that no matter how straight-acting we try to be, we are gender outlaws. Michigan's governor, Jennifer Granholm, after some hard lobbying by Michigan LGBT groups, did the right thing and issued an executive order barring discrimination against transsexual state employees. The Michigan Coalition for Traditional Family Values vowed a fatwa. On Fox News, Sean Hannity's tiny head blew up.

Having upped the gender ante in the presidential race, Hillary is taking hits on prejudices we hardly know we have. Do we really respect her choices as a woman? Do we have to? When the American people shrugged that they did not care what Hillary's husband did sexually in private as long he did his job, it was exactly what gay people have been saying for years. But that whole episode still frosts women. Recently my friend Juan, a big African-American queen and doctor of sociology, tried his gay-male best to explain it to me at dinner.

"Married women have a pact," said Juan, leaning in, PowerPointing with a forkful. "If their husbands cheat on them, they vow they'll leave, especially if the husband embarrasses them publicly. But in fact the women rarely leave, and they hate themselves for their inaction. So there's Hillary, a powerful woman, whose husband cheats on her, gets caught, goes on TV, denies it, and gets impeached. By standing by her man, Hillary is an affront to married women, a reminder of their weakness, a hologram of their self-hatred."

I am not convinced self-hatred is so gendered, but when an older woman in South Carolina stood and asked John McCain, "What are we going to do to beat the bitch?" I did find myself shaking my head, muttering, "Why do you hate yourself so much?" McCain's uncomfortable chuckle suggested that he has thought, heard, or said worse.

Of course, I support Hillary not just as a gender lens and baro-

metric pressure reader of sexism but also as an actual woman with a big laugh, a big brain, and cleavage, for God's sake. I was the first in my neighborhood to sport a "Hillary's First Day: 01.21.09" bumper sticker.

Do not think for a moment that I am not taking all manner of flak for my Hillary support at home. My dear partner loves to out me as a Hillary supporter to friends, family, and elevator guys. She is appalled by Hillary's hawkishness, her equivocation on gay marriage, and her three-day delay in refuting General Peter Pace's claim that homosexuality is immoral.

I agree. Then I paraphrase Donald Rumsfeld right back to her: "You go to the polls with the candidate you have, not the one you wish to have." In 2007 she closed the deal: Hillary is my guy.

........................................................................

## Sitting Shiva on She

### February 2008

Don't ask. I am a sixty-year-old white woman with the last name Clinton. How do you think I feel?

Please do not tell me your long-night-of-the-soul, "Let this cup pass from me, Oprah" story about when you decided to switch from Hillary to Obama. I do not feel your pain.

Please do not send me that "Good-bye to All That (#2)" Robin Morgan piece. It's brill, but it reminds me of one of those desperate prayer chain letters. When you haven't got a prayer. Besides, I am the weakest link in chain letters.

When I ask you a simple question, like "Can we get to Forty-second Street in this traffic?" please do not breathlessly bug-eye me with "Yes, we can!" Sheesh.

Please do not tell me your heartwarming stories about your kids lobbying you to switch to Obama. He is the real deal. He is for change.

He is a great orator. Compared to George Bush, your desk lamp is a great orator. Don't tell. I might look like I am listening, but I am thinking, "Yet another reason not to have children."

Like the new Lexus, I have precollision intelligence, so I did not watch the last Democratic debate. I missed one out of 1,290 of them. Sue me. My partner watched. Actually she switched back and forth between *American Idol* with Simon Cowell and *American Political Idol* with Tim Russert. At least my partner, unlike Hillary's partner, did not announce to everyone that if I did not do well in Ohio and Texas, I would not have a chance. What is that cologne you are wearing, Bill? Passive-Aggressive?

I put on her new Bose headset, cranked up Strauss's "Also Sprach Zarathustra," and did the crossword puzzle.

Did I miss anything?

Obama won? Wow, I so did not see that one coming.

I have been thinking about returning to my radical lesbian separatist roots. Get back to the land. Get off the grid. Get some flannel shirts at Urban Outfitters. Douse myself with some patchouli. Okay, maybe not that far back. But I have been rereading my favorite feminist thinkers.

Like the contemporary French feminist philosopher Monique Wittig. She said that heterosexuality is a political regime in which "woman" exists only through her relation to the category "man." Between Gauloises, she called for the abolition of gender categories and boldly proclaimed that lesbians are not women.

Aha! My mistake was wanting a woman president. Heck, I would like a woman on late-night television. Next time I will be much more specific. I want a lesbian president who is not beholden to a man or the derivative, woman. Think Mike Bloomberg, but *vive la différence*. He bought the NYC mayoralty fair and square, so he did not owe anyone anything. That allowed him to go after smokers, small-gun toters, and trans fats.

Shiva is the paradoxical god of opposites. What is the opposite of the cynicism of despair but the audacity of hope? Where is Christine Quinn? Get me Tammy Baldwin's number.

..................................................................................

# It Ain't Over

**March 2008**

Hillary Clinton is like Glenn Close in *Fatal Attraction*. She just keeps coming back for more. She is a fighter, and you have got to love that. No, really, you have got to love that. Don't make me have to come over there.

She hasn't asked me, but I don't think Hillary should get out of the race. I do think she should take maybe a couple of days off. Go down to Florida, where the state motto, translated from the Latin, is "Where your primary vote does not count either." She should sit in the sun with a big straw hat on and read a big fat Danielle Steel book cover to cover. Chill.

Barack Obama went to the Virgin Islands for Easter break. Well, heck, he could not go to his old church. He played some awesome hoops while Hillary was trying to avoid nonsniper fire. Maybe rope-a-dope is his new strategy.

The campaign has gone on so long we have cycled through seasons of sports metaphors: the symbology of football bowls, basketball bracketology, baseball spring training. Why stop before the Summer Olympics? The torch is on the way from Greece to China by way of Mount Everest, through some got-nothing-to-lose monk riots. Let the games continue!

In a recent poll—and I don't know about you; I can't get enough of those recent polls—38 percent of Democrats said that if their candidate is not the presidential nominee, they are going to vote for McCain. The poll was translated from scratchy Arabic on a cassette tape dropped off at CNN. Does anyone have a GPS reading on Karl Rove?

Based on that poll, everybody, even Fickle Friends of Hillary (FFOH) is calling for Hillary to get out of the race. I even heard someone invoke the name of Tonya Harding. That is cold. Hey, we have

come this far in the presidential marathon, why make Hillary pull a reverse Rosie Ruiz?

Fighters are made better by good sparring partners. Tennis players improve with hard-hitting practice partners. My niece takes her role in practice on her division-leading college lacrosse team very seriously.

If Barack Obama thinks the Clintons are relentless, petty, and dirty double-teamers, I am sure there is a Yogi Berra saying that applies here to indicate that he ain't seen nothing yet.

McCain is a reckless kamikaze for freedom. He has the grudging support of his fellow Republicans and their machine. McCain also has the full-larynxed support of the media boys he has curried for years. They love his ass.

The Loserland television networks are invested in keeping the campaign going, despite their disingenuous goading of Hillary to quit. They say, Do the delegate math. There is no way she can win. They must have forgotten what Harvard's Larry Summers said about women and math.

Like the print media, the networks are hemorrhaging audience to the Internet. This is their last campaign hurrah. And they desperately want to elect one more president for the Gipper.

So Obama/Michael Douglas, quit your whining. Hillary is doing you a favor. Do not be caught flat-footed. Get your cup on. Wear your head and mouth gear.

And watch for her knockout punch.

................................................................................

# Hubble, Hubble

### May 2008

Astronauts have retooled the refractory mirrors on the Hubble telescope. Because the lens had been ground incorrectly, images were disastrously blurry. Think annoying contact lens. The corrections, made by astronauts over several visits to the orbiting telescope, have made

objects in the mirror—well, you know the rest. Now we can see the nose hairs on aliens.

The 2008 presidential primary season reground the mirrors on my old feminist telescope. When it was first installed in me, during the late 1970s, I viewed everything through its lens. I was on duty 24/7. Politics, sports, movies, movie trailers, fashion, education, religion, coworkers, my family and friends. I had a permanent crick in my neck, squint lines around my eyes, and detailed notations in a thick, thumbed record book.

It was hard to maintain that level of observation.

Caroline Herschel, a German astronomer from the late 1700s, discovered nebulae, comets, and planetary satellites. Hershel is usually described as pockmarked and stunted from typhus, and always mentioned in relation to her astronomer brother. She worked until she was ninety-six. Unlike her, I started skipping work shifts.

Maria Mitchell, an American astronomer from the mid-1850s, pioneered data reduction and discovered a comet using a four-foot telescope. Though Mitchell discovered her comet two days before a priest at the Vatican Observatory did, he got all the astro cred and prize money. Unlike her focus, mine drifted.

There was slippage. "He didn't mean it that way." "Those aren't really fuck-me pumps." "At least he didn't kill her." "She's being ironic." "Boys will be boys." "Bitch is a fun rhyme." "Sex sells." "What're you gonna do?" Images and outrages blurred. Once pioneering women astronauts were wearing diapers.

Several events of the primary season sent me to my self-storage area to get out my old telescope. The older white woman's uncontested question to John McCain: "How are we going to beat the bitch?" The Citizens United Not Timid, i.e., CUNT. The Hillarious pantsuits jokes. The interrupted, split-screen coverage of Hillary speeches versus the endless full-screen coverage of Obama speeches.

You will be happy to know that I have just relaunched my kick-ass upgraded telescope, thanks to the booster rocket of my fury. It has settled into its orbit and its clear eye is again trained on Earth. We were going to use infrared sexism detectors, but it made our brilliant blue and green Earthen marble look all Martian red. We had to reboot the intensity filter down a notch. In a fanciful touch, I have etched the SCUM manifesto onto its state-of-the-art aluminum tubing.

Here, let me show you what this little baby can do. See that red splotch? That's Colorado Springs. According to our ship's log, they just had a Father-Daughter Purity Ball. Sponsored by the group the Abstinence Clearinghouse, fathers and their teenage daughters from all over the country gather for a really awkward prom.

Two fathers hold large swords to form an arch before a seven-foot wooden cross. So much for the handmade white Kleenex carnation arbor. Beneath the drawn swords, the fathers make a promise before God "to cover their daughters as authority and protection in the area of purity." Many of the girls just wanted the Mini Cooper convertible. Before I had my telescope reground, I might have thought this a quaint new ritual from a declining mountain tribe.

In fact, many of the girls do have sex before marriage and, more alarmingly, are far less likely to use condoms than their peers. Instead of the prom, the fathers and daughters should have double-dated to *Knocked Up.*

See there? Just down the valley from Colorado Springs, there in Eldorado, Texas? Follow that line. That's the Yearning for Zion Ranch. It is due west of the Crawford, Texas, home of the Bush Yearning for Scion Ranch. High-def, right? You can see they are still cleaning up from the wedding of the Jenna One.

After an anonymous tip from a sixteen-year-old who said that she was being abused by her older husband, child welfare officials raided the self-contained Fundamentalist Church of Jesus Christ of Latter-day Saints compound and removed 465 children. The children were scattered in foster care throughout the state.

What with the price of gas and all, wouldn't it have been much simpler and more to the point to round up the men? I am reminded of Mae West's great words: "Most men want to protect me. Can't figure out from what."

The mothers wear pastel prairie dresses and front-loaded hair. We are told the women leave their hair long so that they can wash the feet of Jesus when he comes again. We nod as if that were a legitimate fashion explanation. HBO, which has given a moral pass to Mafia brutality in *The Sopranos* and to creepy Robin Hood sadomasochism in *Dexter,* has tarted up the oppressive system of FLDS as religious liberty, not licentiousness. It is a divinely inspired system; for the old guys. I am not feeling the Big Love.

Now watch my telescope laser in on that deep blood red in Austria. There in that little town for twenty-four years, in that nondescript house, a father, Josef Fritzi, kept his daughter imprisoned in the basement, where he raped her repeatedly. She birthed seven children by him. One of the most heartbreaking lines of the coverage was "They never saw the light of day." Incredibly, in this Austrian *Upstairs, Downstairs* horror/reality story, his wife raised three other children and claimed to be unaware of what was happening in her basement.

There in France, the red is real. In that private clinic, a doctor is performing a hymenoplasty to "recapture" a young woman's virginity. One Muslim man sued his fiancée's family for breach of contract when he discovered that their daughter, his new wife, had not been chaste. The civil case riveted France. For many Muslim women, the suture restores their future and protects them from certain beatings, even death. So many desperate women seek the restorative surgery that the service is advertised on the Internet and medical tourism packages are available in countries where the procedure is less expensive.

Not only is my new telescope on high red alert, it can connect the dots. The readout I am getting is a globally positioned system based on the dominion of old men over women and young girls, and the ostracism of young boys who pose a competitive threat to the old men.

What to do with all this information? After reconfirmation that the system of sexism had flourished while my attention was elsewhere, my first impulse was to get off the grid, put my telescope back in storage, read some of those new pink chick-lit books, and call it a day.

Instead I am pouring more money into developing and networking with other observers, launching pilotless drones for more accurate on-the-ground information, and inventing a mirror image of that old stealth bomb that killed people and left buildings standing. Ours will be a bomb smart enough to take down the edifice and leave the people standing. We will use our power for good, but this time we will define the Good Parameters System. It is a whole new GPS.

···············································································

# Carpooling on the Straight Talk Express

### June 2008

Newsflash: You are not going to believe this! I just got a call from that darling Caroline Kennedy on the Obama VP search team, and she said they need a sixty-year-old white woman, last name Clinton. Just not that one. Would I be her stunt double? Kidding.

Hillary cannot win. She cannot even win for losing. The night Obama finally hit his lucky number, she was not gracious enough for some of the prissy Miss Mannerses of the press. They wanted groveling, sackcloth, ashes, rending of garments, tearing out of hair. Tears, maybe.

No, wait—not the tears! She might accidentally win another primary. Jesse Jackson dawdled Michael Dukakis for days. Come on.

The night of the last primaries, Hillary won but lost. She said she was not ready to concede, you hideous sexist pigs. She did not say that last part. Someday I would love to have a boilermaker, or eight, with her, up at the house in Chappaqua. She would be doing her hobbies: scrapbooking the campaign, decoupaging war endorsements, gelding Bill and Terry. We would be talking.

But I am projecting. Compared to me, she is the nice Clinton. Bitter? You want bitter? I could give you bitter. But I do not have time.

As I have said, I am a Democratically fluid adult. I will go to the polls with the candidate we have, not the one I wished to have.

Far be it from me to step on anyone's smile. Congratulations, Barack Obama! May you wage a presidential campaign as brilliant as your primary campaign.

Beware the pundits. They need their jobs, so they have to make up stories. Set your own timetable, as you have with your vice presidential choice. And we all know girls do not ask boys to dance. Duh.

Do not ride the Straight Talk Express bus. John McCain will say

"my friend." He is not your friend. Karl Rove is the bus driver. You have the money. Do not carpool with McCain. They will make you sit in back.

The pundits have said, so it must be true, that Obama has to win white non-college-educated voters. Well then, how about giving them no-strings tuition and sending them to college? But they have to guarantee they'll stop watching Fox News.

Already I heard one pundit say that if Obama wants to win, he is going to have to muzzle his wife. Once again, cynicism humps my leg.

# Do You Have to Go?

### June 2008

It is the first Tuesday after the Democratic primaries and it is blistering hot in New York. For days it had been rainy and cool, and then suddenly, perhaps because it is the last days of school and God is a harsh schoolmistress, the weather broke hot like blazes.

We had been out of town, there was no food in the apartment, and we were trying to beat the heat. I was heading to the grocery store. My girlfriend was trying to ride the subway before temperatures on the platform reached Hades levels. It was early. We had been awakened by the sound of our AC laboring like a jet engine at the end of a runway.

We stopped for a quick breakfast. In a few hours the place would be slammed with families, solos, construction workers. The diner decorates for every holiday and seems to have an artist on staff who lovingly paints the windows and interior mirrors with cornucopia scenes, snow scenes, elaborately scrolled holiday greetings, or outsized colored Easter eggs with vaguely Thalidomidic bunnies. The ceiling is a bright, sky-blue convex dome ringed with tiny national flags. It is a cheery permanent homage to the dream of the UN.

One day I was at the crowded breakfast counter when a woman

behind me stretched across us and handed the owner an envelope, saying, "Here it is!" He took it and kissed the envelope, his eyes filling with tears, and he thanked her over and over again to her "No, no, thank you" demurrals.

Someone asked through a mouthful of bagel what was in the envelope. "My son's green card," he exulted. The packed restaurant broke into applause. He explained that the woman was a regular customer and an immigration lawyer and had helped him through the process. We all cheered again. It was an "only in New York, kids, only in New York, Cindy Adams" moment.

Whenever I hand him the check at the cash register, he asks, "Do you have to go?" He says it to everyone, eyes twinkling over the half-glasses teetering crazily on his nose. Today there is no one at the counter. He reaches back, grabs a couple of napkins, pulls a handful of cherries out of a bag, and counts out seven for me, seven for my partner. He talks as we munch on the cherries.

When he was growing up in a small mountain town in Greece, his father had all kinds of trees—cherry, walnut, avocado, lemon, fig. His father told him that if you grow trees, you should let them give you something. He said he would sit in a tree and eat cherries until he made himself sick. During World War II, because so many Greek resistance fighters hid out in the hills, the Germans set fire to sixteen villages. Nothing of his village was left standing, including his father's farm.

The cherries were like madeleines. I told him how I would sneak into our neighbor's tree and then, with cherry juice smeared gluttonously on my face, deny to my mother that I had been eating the neighbor's cherries. He laughed and asked me what I did for a living. My girlfriend and major promoter piped up, "She's a political comic." He beamed and leaned on the counter and opined sadly how the world had been ruined by eight years of Bush. The economy. Our world reputation. The environment.

That is what I talk about, I told him. He said he would come to my show and asked my last name. I said Clinton. I am the last Clinton standing. In a split second, his face went from light and open to dark and closed. He went to the cash register, frowning, shaking his head as he made change I could believe in.

"That woman," he grumbled. "She is my neighbor up in Chappaqua and she's not nice."

"Why? What did she do?" I was thinking that all the cable trucks and secret security details must be a pain in the neighborhood.

"I said hello to her once on the street and she ignored me. She's no good."

We had to go.

Already I had read some article with dire advice from other also-rans about how to handle the inevitable depression that is to come. My local NOW chapter has told me to send her a letter of thanks for all she has done. Who are they, my mother? Of course I will, but I am not bugging her for a couple days.

On this hot, ordinary Tuesday morning, I hope Hillary Clinton slept in, put on her bathrobe, padded downstairs for coffee in her own hair and with no makeup, did not read any papers or watch any TV, and maybe just sat quietly and watched peonies bloom in the backyard.

I wish her a day at a diner, when she can sit at a counter, order a piece of cherry pie and a coffee, and not have someone resent or second-guess her or give her apple pie because he knows that is what she really meant.

Thank you.

## The Itch to Hitch

### June 2008

Happy Summer Solstice! And Merry Christmas while I am at it, because that is how fast time is flying.

It is Day #14 of my Hillary withdrawal. For at least seventeen months I saw her every day, knew where she was going, who she was having dinner with—now nothing. It feels like a sad, if amicable, breakup. Now we have to start seeing other people. Sigh.

Perhaps the biggest shock upon coming out of the Democratic primary bubble is realizing that I had been lulled into thinking that everybody was now trying to work in an adult, democratic, progressive, civic manner. Silly me.

Out in the unreal world of Bushland, George and John Cocaine, his Mini-Me, want to drill their bits into every inch of Mother Earth. They are squeezing the last little bit of speculative oil out before His Category 43ness leaves. They are back to photo-opping on broken levees. They are ignoring Iraq's ungrateful but fond wish for us to leave, now that it is going so well. ("For whom?" being the unasked question.) They are spreading manure lies about Barack HUSSEIN Obama's religious beliefs. They are going after Michele Obama, who is resisting their demands for an extreme makeover.

In short, they got nuthin' but fear and hate, their two favorite cards.

Happily, I have been following a different Haight. Despite the flagrant flaunting and taunting from California friends—"Sooooo, when are you two getting married?"—my gal pal and I recently reconfirmed our own vows not to marry. We do, however, vigorously support the freedom of others to marry.

While we do not have the itch to hitch, we cannot get enough of our friends' lovely stories of all the weddings in California. With gas at $4.65 a gallon in L.A., I encourage newlyweds to locate their bridal registries at the local gas station.

And na na na na na na, back at you, California—one word: Celtics. And so much for that illusion of grownup behavior.

Our Empirical State is making progress. When Governor David Paterson issued an executive order that New York State must recognize out-of-state marriages, he spoke lovingly of the early influence of his two gay uncles, Stanley and Ronald. Reverend Al Sharpton teased him that he might have unwittingly outed them. Paterson said he was only disappointed that Rosie O'Donnell had not called him. With any luck, Paul Rudnick is already writing a sequel—*In & Out, Part II*. I am working on *Same Sex and the City*.

Happy Summer of Love! What do you want for Christmas, besides a First Lady Obama?

# Faith-Based Comedy

I denounce all pastors. I was denouncing before denouncing was cool. I denounce Jerry Falwell in absentia for all the harm his words still wreak on young gay people. I denounce Praise the Lord's Pat Robertson and his shar-pei smile. I denounce James Dobson from the Colorado Springs group Fuck Us on the Family. I denounce his hateful cousin Lou Dobbs in his anti-immigrant bullying pulpit on CNN. I denounce the Huckabee smarm. I denounce Joel Osteen, God's show pony and patron saint of teeth whitener, who announced that he did not think homosexuality was God's best effort. Do not get me started on the pope. It is not the religions I denounce, it is their fundamentalisms. I give great props to openly gay Bishop Gene Robinson of New Hampshire. I support freedom for and from religion. Praying should be like doing your Kegel exercises: no one needs to know you are doing it and you achieve lovely results. I am a radical secularist pluralist. God speaks through me too. PTL—Praise the Lesbians.

# The Sistine Shusher

## July 2005

Great news! I have identified my next career. I had always planned to become a librarian after I retired from being a comedian. After years of trying to make people laugh loudly, I thought it would be fun to go around, index finger to pursed lips, bug-eyeing people into silence. Ironically, librarians are some of the loudest, staunchest supporters of free speech, so my activist needs would also be met. But with Amazon and Google, people do not go to libraries much anymore, and I do not do house calls, so I despaired of ever finding a second career.

After a delightful Greek cruise with Olivia's offshore lesbians, we were in Italy when I found my next vocation. It was quite a culture shock to go from seven days of feeling free with my sea gals to plunging into the art and commerce of Italy. I tried to preserve that lovely presumption of lesbianism for as long as I could. We like to think the best of everyone. When the voice on my self-guided-tour headset kept telling me to admire the quick, deft brushstrokes of painting #47 without ever commenting on the grisly content of the rape of the Sabine women or the massacre of the innocents in lurid but well-executed detail in #49, I knew the illusion was over.

At first we were cheered by the faded rainbow *PACE* flags strung from Roman balconies, but they were more about peace than gay trendsetters. We oriented our gay positioning systems, found the gay bookstore, and asked Claudio, the very patient manager, where all the gay people were. In English far better than my ciao-Prego-Ragu Italian, he explained that the closet there was huge, churchlike—that there was a gay village Tuesday nights, six euros entrance fee, and that the Rome gay pride march was the next weekend. Given the new pope, Claudio said, the march was more important than ever.

We were unable to get an audience with said new pope and Harry Potter hater, the Widow Ratzinger, but I now know why those zip-off

pants/shorts were invented. No sleeveless shirts, no shorts, no service with the pope. Since we had papal time to spare, we toured the Vatican. More marble busts of men with no eyes. More steroidal statues of ancient circuit party men. More tapestries of striving, sandaled men, glowering Russell Crowe–like, throwing the phone at the front desk. Finally we reached the stifling Sistine Chapel, mobbed with touristas hailing the very gay frescoed ceiling with their upturned cell phone/cameras, their yakking towering to a muted roar.

Suddenly a hissing, sibilant, sharp *SHHHH!* stopped the din mid-Babel. The Sistine Shusher! It was as if the crowd had received a holy bee-otch slap. When the bedlam built again, the Shusher slapped it down again. That is the job for me. Of course I would secularize it. Instead of *shush*, I would do a shushing *sheesh*. "We do not have a litmus test for Supreme Court vacancies." *Sheesh!* "We do not know where that leak came from, do we, Kardinal Karl?" *Sheesh!* "We remain steadfast and confident in the war on terror." *Sheesh!*

I am just practicing, but I feel better already. This job has health benefits!

........................................................................

# Reading Between the Holy Lines
## March 2006

I am not saying this in any kind of *Mayflower* snooty way, but I was recently jiggering with some of those nifty Mormon genealogy computer programs and have traced my lineage back through Saint Bridget to Mary Magdalene and Jesus. I do not mean to brag, but it turns out I have Jesus's cheekbones. For a couple of extra dollars, I also found that my partner, a goddess of multitasking, is a direct descendant of the many-armed and dangerous Hindu goddess Kali.

Despite our luminous lineage, we would not be allowed to adopt a child in the Boston Archdiocese of Mormon Mitt's Massachusetts.

Apparently the 2003 Vatican statement that same-sex adoptions are "gravely immoral" and "would actually mean doing violence to these children" was not trumped by the trumpeted 2006 papal encyclical "Deus Caritas Est," or "God Is Love." In his first official papal letter, after the semiofficial papal Post-it "Harrium Potterum Anti-Christum Est," Benedict XVI mused to the faithful on the glories of love.

The papal apologists at the *New York Times* expressed surprise in their article on the encyclical that the pope did not denounce the abomination of gay marriage. They seemed unwilling to read between the holy lines when the pope went on and on about the sacred rightness of the love between a man and a woman.

But P.P.S., papal post scriptum, what does His Papal Red Prada Pumpiness know of love? With those deep-set eyes, was he a big dater before seminary? Does he have a secret stash of Harlequin romances? Is Danielle Steel soon to be on the fast track to sainthood? Is he actually admitting that unmarried priests really are loveless losers? Does he have a pull-string doll of Jack Nicholson saying to Helen Hunt in *As Good as It Gets,* "You make me a better man"?

Though the evangelist John wrote, "God is love, and he who abides in love abides in God, and God abides in him," holy smokescreen, there are some exceptions to all that abiding. When the state of Massachusetts required the church to follow antidiscrimination laws in order to receive public dollars, the Boston Archdiocese stopped doing adoptions altogether.

The new pope, Benedict, makes the old pope, John Paul, seem as benign as Mr. Magoo. He is intent on winnowing and purifying his flock. He holds a tight rein on his shepherds, who seem eager to do his bidding, and he is removing any hint of brokebacklash from the herd.

Newsflash to gay Catholics: The church hates your guts. No matter the goodness in your lineage. Be mindful if your host or wine tastes a little funny. I would suggest not sitting in the front pew. I would suggest leaving.

......................................................................................

# Ding-Dong

## May 2007

I remember exactly where I was when I heard that Jerry Falwell had died. I had just landed from a cross-country flight and was in a taxi, trying to preserve the pleasure of a six-hour newsless cocoon, when I heard on the radio, ". . . delays on the upper span of the George Washington, the Nets won one at home, and Reverend Jerry Falwell is dead." My cabbie did not know the words to "Ding-Dong, the Witch Is Dead" and seemed mystified when I abruptly stopped my cater-wauling rendition and apologized to him for the insult to those good witches.

As more of our homophobic nemeses die, and not a moment too soon, I don my Miss Gay Manners pince-nez and humbly recommend one gay etiquette guideline about how best to respond. The old gray-haired white guys with the first names Reverend, Pope, and Billy are aging out, dying off, happily disproving the theory "He's just too mean to die." Like George Bush, they are all concerned about their legacy and seem to have left sons and scions, Mini-Mes of meanness. Before the next gen of ex-gay proselytizers assume the position, let's have a moment of silence.

Okay, that's enough.

Reactions to the news of Falwell's death varied wildly. Some went scurrilous. Faster than you can say Tinky Winky, those reactions were quickly spotted in the deep blogosphere. One suspects they were pre-written. Apparently everyone had archived the video of Jerry rocketing down the water slide at the old PTL park. The "What would Jesus douche?" comments were unnecessary.

Some went nice. Those columns were granted syndicated sanction, as Falwell's former foes tried mightily to say the good things they had learned from jousting with Jer. We can love the sinner and hate the sin better than you can any day, etc. They seemed in their own po-

lite way to be trying to adhere to the caution of Moms Mabley: "You have to say good things about the dead. He's dead. Good."

Though they tried mightily, their comments were quickly countered by the army of Jerry's kids claiming that their dear leader did not hate gay people. No, see, he was trying to save us from acting on our gayness and going straight to hell. Except for Ann Coulter. She hates everything.

Moderation, as always, is key in these situations. Before the whooping cries of relief and glee, the backslapping congratulations, the celebratory bonfires, I recommend a three-day waiting period. This is a quiet time, perhaps used for purchasing rainbow bunting. This valuable cooling-off period, seldom used when purchasing a gun in Virginia, for example, is essential to avoid embarrassment. What if you are in the midst of a dancing-on-his-grave performance piece and get word that miraculously Jerry has come again, rolled back the stone, seen his enormous bulbous shadow, and it is seventy-three more years of gay-bashing? What then?

But by my calculation, three days have passed, and I just finished blow-drying my papier-mâché Tinky Winky with the big Jerry Falwell head! Good.

................................................................................

# Ordained Comic

### February 2008

One Sunday morning I was doing my usual pro forma plow through the pages of the *New York Times Magazine* to get to the crossword puzzle. After a pleasant stop at "The Ethicist" and a swipe at the mysterious-to-me "Funny Page," I was dutifully page-turning, pretending I cared, when I happened on the article "Did You Hear the One About the Christian Comedian?" The comedian of interest is Anita Renfroe, aka the "William Tell Mom," if you are looking for her oeuvre on YouTube, where she is a huge sensation.

Oh God, not another in-depth article about women and humor. After years of sparse coverage, this was the second extended mainstream piece on women and humor in two months. I was still thinking about Alessandra Stanley's *Vanity Fair* piece "Who Says Women Aren't Funny?" Why is it that every statement about women and humor has to be framed as a question? Her "So there, Christopher Hitchens" was understood.

Despite the interesting work of the highlighted women comics and her own best efforts, for the bulk of the article Stanley fell back on the standard trope to analyze women comics: the pretty-is-to-funny ratio. Annie Liebovitz did the accompanying photo shoot with the women tarted up to look like the "high-end" prostitutes the difficult former governor of New York must have been looking for. Amy, Maya, Tina as the über Ashley Alexandra Dupré. They put the ho in ho-ho.

Just as people have a mental image of "lesbian comic"—large, loud, flannel—I pictured a "Christian comedian" as Dana Carvey's purse-lipped "isn't that special" church lady, but without the orthopedic, form-fitting moon shoes.

Renfroe is a curvy forty-five-years old, a mom, and a Christian from Cobb County, Georgia. At first I thought we were about as different as two women can be and would be beelining it to the crossword puzzle. I kept reading.

Because, in fact, if you substituted "lesbian" for "Christian," not only would you risk eternal damnation, but you would also see how much Anita and I have in common. Think sinful synchronicity.

Anita's career challenge has been to prove that being a Christian comedian is not an oxymoron. When I began to perform, I called myself a fumerist, i.e., a feminist-humorist. What was originally a typo became an amazing gimmick. I am convinced I did more than my share of drive-time radio interviews because the disk jockeys always had to meet the "fumerist" and ask, at five-thirty a.m., "Feminist-humorist? Isn't that an oxymoron?" I would say, "You're half right."

Anita's other task has been to prove that liberation from womanly woes could come through a deeper relationship with Jesus Christ. My job has been to show that women's liberation comes through a deeper relationship with feminism.

Anita got her comic chops coming up through the ranks of small

church appearances. I did too. I will always be grateful for the Unitarian church basements rented by my early producers. I knew I had arrived when I got to perform upstairs in the big room. To this day I say a prayer of gratitude to the Unit.

From her humble beginnings, Anita began playing multicity tours produced by the Women of Faith Circuit. She began to make a living performing and selling her CDs, DVDs, and books after each show. I came up through a large underground circuit of lesbian coffeehouses and conferences and then played huge music and comedy festivals. I always sold and signed product after shows.

The description of the two-day Christian conference called "Amazing Freedom," with its women-only audience numbering in the thousands, aswoon from being together and hearing songs and jokes about their lives, is the same, minus the nudity and tabouli, as that of a Michigan Womyn's Music Festival. And I bet "Amazing Freedom" does not allow male-to-female transgender people in either.

Anita was raised a Baptist in the small Texas town of Burnett. She said her faith culture was not fond of funny and was all about what you could not do. I was raised a Catholic in upstate New York. My faith culture was Catholic fundamentalism. My mother attended daily mass. We often said the family rosary after dinner. My goal during those recitations was, without visible prompts, to get my oldest brother to fall to the floor, laughing helplessly. I received the sacraments in a timely fashion. I went to Catholic schools from first grade through college.

Like Anita's, my faith has provided me with hours of material. My comic point of view was forged in reaction to the sexism I experienced as an out-of-work altar girl and budding lesbian. Catholic taboos were my to-dos.

Anita is at a career crossroads. She is a funny woman who happens to be a Christian. Can she cross over to the mainstream? I pray to God she can because there is a definite stained-glass ceiling in the church. No matter how much the church PR guys in the nutty hats want their clients to say "Mother Church," their brand is still the church of the holy father, the patriarchy. Anita is like Saint Joan Rivers, martyred on the cross of the real question for women in comedy: "Who do you think you are?"

At least my church of feminism actually wants me around. Especially after Betty Friedan's "purple menace" proclamation got shouted down by all the dyke deacons running the darned thing. Contrary to the threatened whine of the men at the time, the women's movement had a sense of humor, and when we were not laughing at the guys, we were ignoring them. They felt left out. That made them say insulting things, like we did not have a sense of humor.

Anita says she never wanted to be a minister, but her comedy is clearly her ministry. She loves her job, the high of making women laugh. Her message of empowerment is essentially the same as feminism. It is humor toward something. She likes to leave her audiences with an inspirational, homiletic message. She ended one concert with "Each day you have a choice—hilarity or insanity."

For years I have called myself a faith-based comic who happens to be a lesbian, grateful for every chance to make my living making women laugh. I do think there is something sacred when two or more have gathered together and not asked for comps. I too like to leave an audience with a laugh and a message. My simple exhortation is not as dialectic as Anita's: Be Bad.

# M'Kay?
## April 2008

Now that everyone can shoot cell-phone or flip-cam videos and pop them on YouTube, maybe God, chief all-seeing enforcer of good behavior, can delegate more to iGod. Kick back and relax a bit. Maybe see some baseball. Take a nice bubble bath. Have a flavored European-style coffee.

Remember George Allen's "macaca" moment? This new citizen surveillance makes the Bush wiretapping seem like pinning clothes onto a frayed string between tin cans.

Republican representative Sally Kern, from Oklahoma, was re-

cently recorded at a district fundraiser explicating the homosexual agenda. In the audio recording she sounds like Mr. Mackey, the South Park guidance counselor, who ends sentences with a nasal "m'kay?" As cutlery and dishes clank in the background, Ms. Kern tells her peacefully masticating listeners that homosexuality is a bigger threat than terrorism or Islam, which is pretty big, m'kay?

It sounded like a dinner theater performance nightmare I had once. The audience munched contentedly and was completely passive as Ms. Kern listed gay outrages. Gays are recruiting children two years of age. That is why they want early childhood education. They are infiltrating city councils in Florida and even Eureka Springs, where they have that Passion play, m'kay? Homosexuality is like cancer in your little toe. It is deadly and spreading. It is not a healthy lifestyle. Gay life spans are shorter because of suicides, illness, and discouragement.

Ms. Kern said she was not antigay or gay-bashing. She also noted presciently and accurately that even talking like this could put her in jeopardy. Nevertheless, she plowed on courageously, m'kay? The audio of her talk was posted, whipsawed around the Internet, and picked up briefly by CNN. Many gay organizations and their allies are demanding her removal.

But otherwise Ms. Kern's comments and the murder of Lawrence King, a gay middle-schooler in Oxnard, California, barely make news. After being the wedge issue in many of the last elections, the eerie silence on LGBT issues in this current campaign has been unsettling. "Go to my Website" is not an acceptable candidate explanation for the absence of LGBT issues.

While some of my colleagues prefer getting things done below the radar, like my personal saint, Mae West, I have always felt it is better to be looked over than overlooked.

God is kicking back. Through His spokesman here on earth, Pope Benedict (don't tell W.!), He released a newly upgraded list of sins of the globalized world at a Lenten Apostolic Penitentiary Seminar.

The pope had PowerPointed the more venial sins of road rage, drunkenness, and rudeness in an earlier address last summer. It is unclear if he had any papal input in the new Italian law that men cannot fondle their own genitals through their clothes in public. The pope himself prefers layers.

The Lenten trade show was a major bummer at the Vatican't. Some

of the lowlights: Presentations showed that 60 percent of Catholics in Italy no longer go to confession; a graph showed that today's secularized world has a decreasing sense of sin; and increasing numbers of people in the secularized West are making doo-doo without God.

Pope Benedict, sporting those devilish Prada pumps, addressed the Vatican body. Employing impeccable *ex cathedra* logic, the papal plan is to get people back to confession with a whole new class of upgraded sins. There are now even more ways to offend God! And sinning is not just for individuals anymore. Sins now have "social resonance."

Think social networking but with hell time. I know I do. It was not clear if confessionals would be renovated for higher occupancy.

The new mortal sins are not to be replacements for the traditional one-word individualistic sins of pride, envy, gluttony, lust (Eliot Spitzer did not get that memo), anger, greed, and, my personal favorite, sloth. They are additional multiword sins like carrying out morally debatable scientific experiments, taking or dealing in drugs, and excessive accumulation of wealth. They sound scarier in the Latin.

The punishments for the single-word sins are well known. Pride: broken on the wheel. Envy: put in freezing water. Catholics have been waterboarding for years. We call it baptism. Gluttony: forced to eat rats, toads, and snakes. Lust: smothered in fire and brimstone. Poor Eliot. Anger: dismembered alive. Greed: put in cauldrons of boiling oil. Sloth: thrown in snake pits. Simple and strict.

Nowhere have I read about the sin of making wicked fun of the pope and all his works. Yet. So I offer new, socially resonant punishment suggestions:

Drug pushers: forced to attend a daily Narcotics Anonymous meeting. Rush L. is in your home group, and he will not stop cross-talking.

Obscenely rich: you and your geeky cohorts must ring the opening and closing bell at the New York Stock Exchange for the rest of your born days.

Polluters: run the Crocs kiosk at the Atlanta airport. The one next to a loud Rosetta Stone Tower of Babel kiosk.

Morally debatable scientific experimenters: forced to judge science fairs at Christian middle schools.

Abortionists: forced to move to Binghamton, New York, home of Randall Terry.

Pedophiliacs: all of the above, including single-word-sin punishments.

I confess to quickly scanning the papal list, looking for the sin of homosexuality. It was not there! Maybe it is understood. It was like being dropped from the big annual *Papal Magazine* "Sinniest Sins Alive" special double issue. For a while there, homosexuality was like being cover-boy Matthew McConaughey doing his buff beach work-out. *Nunc nihil.*

Holy mysterious ways! Thanks to Sally Kern for keeping us in the press, m'kay?

## St. Alf's Science Fair

### May 2008

Faster than you can say, "California Supreme Court Overturns Ban on Gay Marriage," his Extreme Slippery Slopeheadedness Pope Benedict had an announcement to make. Barely taking the time to translate it from the Latin, in that oddly high voice, the pope restated the church's position that only unions between a man and a woman are moral.

In his text, the pope did not mention the California ruling. He just happened to be addressing family groups in Europe. What are the chances? The California ruling and the papal announcement—it was a news-cycle secular mashup miracle!

In another holy coinkydink, the same day the pope condemned gay marriage, another story broke. The Reverend José Gabriel Funes,

in an interview titled "The Extraterrestrial Is My Brother," announced that faith in God did not contradict faith in alien life. As usual, no word on extraterrestrial sisters.

Funes said that one of the themes near and dear to the the Widow Ratzinger's papacy is the relationship between faith and reason. The big bang theory is the most reasonable theory of the creation of the universe and yet it does not contradict the idea that God probably was the guy who pushed down the handle on the explosive box.

Funes is the director of the Vatican Observatory, which in addition to doing top-notch research has a meteorite collection that is one of the best in the world. Hence that old line, "Hey, young fella, want to come up and see my meteorite collection?"

The church is still smarting from its shoddy treatment of Galileo four hundred years ago. It was no picnic for Galileo either. As an independent astronomer, Galileo had brazenly declared that the sun, not the earth, not even the Vatican, is the center of the universe. Funes said that mistakes were made.

The Catholic Church treats homosexuals as an alien life form, a bivalve of being and doing. You can be gay, but you just cannot do anything about it. That is like saying, "You can be a priest, you just cannot say mass." Even though we are alien, we cannot catch a break. Despite the recent announcement, queers have not been upgraded to the church's brother or sister status.

The pope and his faithful boy pals would reason that if Alf were gay, the church would love him, but not if he married Mork. That would be immoral. Alf could marry Mindy. That would be cross-species and a little gross, but definitely still moral.

The pope still has work to do in his Faith and Science Project. If they want to get faith and science back together, it stands to reason that they could start by fusing gay being and doing back together.

........................................................................................

# The Closet and the Confessional
## July 2008

My dad and I were watching *Perry Mason*. My mom was not there. Though she loved whodunits, she could care less who did it. Her expertise was the modus operandi. During every show, just before the killer broke down and confessed, she would interject, eyes never leaving the television, "Watch. He did it because he loved her." And sure enough the guy would sob, "But I loved her." Without looking at me, she winked, vindicated. "See that?"

Is it any wonder I'm gay?

Even then I had no crime-story aptitude. I am *CSI: Deficient.* For all the times I have watched *Charade,* I still do not know who did it. Nor do I care. I got the homo gene, not my mother's m.o. gene. I do know, however, from studying the glorious Audrey Hepburn, the art of seamlessly tying a scarf around my head and neck. Perfectly. Audrey is the cause of my lasting obsession with large sunglasses.

During *Perry Mason,* I was most interested in Perry's loyal assistant, the curvy, efficient, and delicious Della Street. I grew impatient with the story.

"That guy did it. Why doesn't he just tell them?"

"Because the show would be over."

"But that's lying."

My father patted my head absentmindedly, "Because he doesn't want to go to jail."

I was stunned.

Lying was a sin. Murder was a sin. Even thinking about murder was a sin.

I was on Sig-Alert for sins. In my Catholic grammar school, Sts. Peter and Paul, we were in heavy prep for our first confession. My first-grade pals and I and were like tiny rabbinical students parsing and debating the words of the blue Baltimore catechism.

After confession we would be cleared for communion. I looked forward to being part of the drama-laden solemn public spectacle. In my pre–Vatican II church, girls were completely cut out of altar boy performance art. While my altar boy brothers struggled to learn their measly few lines, I learned to say an entire mass, in Latin, at my secret altar down in our basement catacomb. I practiced swinging my incense censer for hours in the basement. Instead of frankincense, I burned wads of tea leaves. I served grape juice.

For my first Holy Communion, I planned to play a Shirley Temple "little angel" role with a trace of *Song of Bernadette*. My mother made my dress. When one of my co-celebrants in her ridiculous frothy white confection sniffed, "Your mother made your dress?" I shot back, "Yes, and there's tender loving care in every stitch." I could have snapped her neck. I would have preferred a simple white suit, even if it was a hand-me-down from my brother, who had made his first Holy Communion the year before.

Truth be told, I would have preferred an off-white cowboy outfit, with fringing appropriate for the ceremony. My mom could have made it. She was fearless. She made drapes, slipcovers, and, once, a disastrous bathing suit for my horrified ingenue of a teen sister. One Easter my mom made a cape for me from an unflatteringly stiff blue-and-pink-squared fabric that I suspected was meant to cover my chubby self. Whenever I wore it, I put my white gloved hands out the front arm slits only as far as my wrists and pretended I was an adorable poster child for birth defects.

Mom would have been a *Project Runway* addict. She tried to hand down the family skills to me. But my favorite activity at her Singer sewing machine was to tie a thread from the bobbin to a wooden spool and drag it to some remote place in the house, return to the machine, hit the motor, and listen to the spool bounce and clunk back through the house to me at base camp.

We went to Mr. Sheer's fabric store. He was the first and only Jew of my childhood. His store was crammed floor to ceiling with bolts of fabric, fascinating accessories—a dusty, airless firetrap. We pored over the waxy pages of huge pattern books: Vogue, Butterick, McCall's. Betsy McCall was my first pinup girl. The whoosh of the slowly turning pages lifted my bangs slightly. My mother was looking at the out-

fits the little girls were wearing. I was looking at the little girls. When she asked the magic question, "Do you like this one?" I thought, "I love her! Can I take her home?" but nodded silently.

My communion dress was a simple white cotton eyelet with a satin waistband and a sheer veil held in place in my thickly braided hair with bobby pins, not a headband. This was before glue guns. This was also before the Heimlich maneuver, and my big worry was choking or accidentally touching the host with even the tip of my tongue.

I learned how to pry the soggy, gluten host gently from the roof of my mouth. I will always thank Mother Church for teaching me those nifty tongue movements

But before the public communal ritual of my first Holy Communion, I had to go through the private personal rite of my first confession. I was not looking forward to telling my sins to our grumpy old German pastor, Monsignor Veight, who always laid on the horn when he backed his big black Cadillac out of the rectory garage into the playground, interrupting our jump-rope with me as the designated twirler. I was a horrible jumper. I would lean in, lean in, lean in, timing my entrance jump as I had seen the other girls do, hop in, and get garroted by the rope. Those brush burns on my neck were not hickeys.

Spinning the rope while admiring my girlfriends' footwork and their billowing uniform skirts was hypnotic. The old guy's horn broke my trance. I blew a wet raspberry just as the monsignor's face in the window pulled even with mine. He dragged me to the principal's office for insubordination. Thankfully, I had not learned how to flip the bird.

I really did not think I had any sins to tell. I had a hard enough time buying that we were born defective, with a big black mark of original sin on our souls. It seemed unfair, a "wait until your father comes home" method of control.

The big criterion for sin was doing something intentionally to hurt Jesus. I would never do that. I really did not ever feel I knew the guy. Try as I might. I used to press my knuckles hard into my eyes to induce pyrotechnic colors, then look quickly at the statue of the Blessed Mother. I wanted a vision like those of the tween saints and martyrs we had been studying.

Of course, I had done lots of things intentionally to hurt my three brothers, but most of that involved payback. And I did that cruel thing with that Easter cape. I had given a Bronx cheer to our monsignor, but it was instinctual, not intentional. The whole intentionality vetting left a lot of loopholes for a little rationalizer like myself. Later in life, I found the Golden Rule much more helpful: Do unto others as you would have them do unto you. It was the Baltimore Catechism for Dummies.

But there was no first communion without a first confession. So on a frosty morning we filed over to the dark, deserted church, still smelling faintly of incense from a funeral earlier. We were all tense. One girl threw up in her prayerfully folded hands. I stood in the long snaking line of young sinners, and we all watched as the recently confessed slid back the thick red curtain and emerged, squinting, slightly stunned, into the dim light. I tried to read them for signs of new holiness.

When my turn came, I trudged forward, dry-mouthed, ducked past the curtain, and knelt on the unpadded kneeler. I waited, heart thudding in the dark. My eyes adjusted. I was three dizzying inches away from an intricate screen. A door slid open and I could just make out the unearthly white of Monsignor V.'s nearly bald head. He grunted, gave me a tomahawk-chop air blessing, and I began.

My confession was a sin template, a Bad Libs fill-in-the-blanks tearsheet. I used it for years, until I stopped going to confession altogether. "Bless me, father, I disobeyed my parents ____ times. I got angry at my brothers ____ times. I lied ____ times." The monsignor did not cross-examine. My penance was five Hail Marys. I felt I got off easy. Another blessing, more like a sign from a third-base coach. Dismissed. The window slid closed. I walked out.

Though there was no whooping it up in church, no tossing of mantillas in the air after our graduation from sinfulness, my co-confessees seemed quietly relieved as we were marched back to school. My first confession provided no relief. I had hedged.

Even though I knew there would be at least purgatory time for me, I had not mentioned coveting my neighbor's leggy, Sea & Skied, sunbathing wife. It was a sin. I could not imagine how it was in the "hurt Jesus" category, but it was unequivocally one of the Ten Com-

mandments, for God's sake. Though it was number ten on the list, in my backward Catholicism, the commandments might as well have started there. It was enlightened that the framers of my religious constitution were able to separate coveting into nine and ten, property and wives. I guess. I would have preferred the covet cover. I thought the tenth commandment had my name on it.

Thou shalt not covet thy neighbor's wife, Kathleen Ann Clinton. Yes, you.

Every time I read it, I grew hot with shame. I tried to skip it, but I knew it was there. I wanted my neighbor's wife. I also wanted Della Street. I wanted my jump-roping friends, especially the dazzling Virginia Hamel. I wanted some butch outfits to go a-courting. I wanted Mary Martin/Peter Pan. I wanted Julie Andrews. Both Hepburns. I was a nonstop coveter.

Not only did confession not offer full relief, it compromised my later entrance into the community of communicants. What should have been a gateway ritual into full church citizenship was a brokered secret deal. I felt like a fraud. I was sure I got the placebo host.

The confessional's promise of release from the bondage of secrets actually came to me much later, when I came out of the closet. I approached coming out with the same trepidation as confession. At the time there was no such thing as a coming-out group preparation class, no supporting rituals or large institutional support. There were not even any TV specials with Diane Sawyer midwifing a star's coming out.

I practiced my speech. Though the lead-up to coming out had been similar to that of confession, with its shame and dread, this time I did not hedge. I said the magic word for my full redemption. "I am a lesbian." I told a friend. She gave me a whooping, welcoming embrace: "Finally!" No door slid closed in my face. At last I felt the power of transformative release promised by a good confession. That honesty also allowed me full participation in the LGBT community, which supported and frankly admired my coveting.

# *Moral Footprints*

Revolutions have three stages—they become movements, then institutions, and, finally, rackets. The Stonewall Revolution became the LGBT movement. When the fly-by-night, seat-of-their-fashionable-pants, forty-year-old sexual identity movement so threatened the two-thousand-year-old Christian identity movement, we achieved institutional status. We are at a crossroads now. Despite disputes about transgender inclusion and gay marriage strategies, I am optimistic. While apathetic gays whine about gay apathy, I meet young, delightfully entitled gay activists and retired gay people with activist time on their hands. I meet rabid straight allies in Parents and Friends of Lesbians and Gays, Planned Parenthood, and the ACLU. We have our own Gay Mafia now, but our racketeering is the effort to connect with the wider global LGBT challenge and with other movements for social justice, all the while insisting on and assisting the simple, courageous, truth-to-power revolutionary act of coming out.

# Gayvolution Theory

## October 2005

Great news, everyone! I have figured out how to deep-six that de-testable, untestable, pseudoscientific, time-wasting, national embar-rassment of a non-theory called Intelligent Design. George W. Bush recently mused in an interview that ID should be taught in schools along with the theory of evolution, so that no child would be left be-hind later in life when the cocktail party chat turns to "How the bleep did we get here?"

Leaving aside the uproarious notion that George, from George-ville, population: George, should even be allowed to discuss intelli-gence or design, let alone both, his "thinking" shows some . . . well, evolution.

As you know, incurious George once remarked, "The jury is still out on evolution." If he had come to this conclusion after seeing *March of the Penguins,* I might cut him some slack. The movie, so straight, with an unrelenting emphasis on reproduction and monogamy and heartwarming depictions of male penguins caring for their young (for three months of the year), could be a Penguin Family Values DVD bulk-mailed to megachurches everywhere, but it is no brief for evolu-tion. For millions of years, penguins have parked themselves seventy miles from the nearest protein bar and have not perfected the unpro-tected egg toss—nor have they introduced pastels. The jury is left out in the cold. More likely, George, he who sees the world in black and white, watched that snuff documentary *Grizzly Man.*

So why the change in his "thinking"? He seems to have discov-ered that the Scopes trial was not a blind test for mouthwash. His social Darwinism, with its southern strategy of survival of the fittest, has not morphed into a scientific Darwinism. Chances are, it was not from reading about Darwin's finches. For George's "thinking" to have evolved from creationism's cretinous insistence on nothing older than

four thousand years, I speculate someone must have bullet-pointed for him that it takes millions of years to create crude oil.

The flat-earth foolishness of creationism has been forced to evolve into the hybrid theory called Intelligent Design. "The world was made by God" has morphed into "The universe was created by the Grand Designer." Which is so gay. I think God, the wink-wink, nudge-nudge grand designer, is gay, but that was discussed in a previous sermonette.

Intelligent Design is the gayest theory since that darling irrational exuberance. Gay and lesbian people have mysteriously propagated for thousands of years without benefit of hand-me-down DNA. The only identifying genetic tag seems to be an orange Abercrombie & Fitch tab and an ur-tendency toward multipocketedness. And all that can mutate inexplicably next spring. Somewhere in Vietnam there is a woman sewing on a fourteenth pocket, asking, "Why?"

When we propagate now, we do not necessarily produce gay offspring. We have thrived and multiplied amid the most deleterious of conditions. We are magically known to each other through pheromones or feral moans. Despite hypothalamic studies, finger measurements, and gay designer-gene mappings, scientists cannot explain definitively what makes some lucky people gay. We just are.

That mysterious, magical *je ne sais quoi*–ness is the unprovable crux of Intelligent Design. Intelligent Design is gay. Name it and claim it. Loudly and often. Unlike us, it will be gone in six months.

...........................................................................................................

# I Wish I Could Quit Ewe
### January 2007

Reading the *New York Times* in the morning at our house is a contact sport. The day after the State of the Union speech always promises lots of body and paper slamming. George's SOU speech invariably has a

Ground Hog Day, déjà vu quality about it. He appears in late January, and it is twenty more months of nuclear winter.

Before we could even get to the recap, the rehash of his "If I Did It" speech, a headline caught my eye: "Gay Sheep: Science and the Perils of Bad Publicity." It did not take much, and I was off and running. "How dare they call us sheep? We have done more courageous things in one year of our lives than they could ever dream to do in their whole lives! You just try to come out to your parents! You go to your church and hear yourself described as sinner, abomination! You try being out at work. Or out of work, because you are gay. You are the sheep. When you are not being chickens. You are so sheepish, you should all be drinking Woolite cosmos down at your special cafés! Last year it was *Brokeback* jokes—now this."

Coffee was flying. I punctuated each statement by slamming the paper on the comforter.

My girlfriend let me run on a bit and then pointed out, her Jane Curtin to my Roseanne Roseannadanna, that the article was about a study of actual gay sheep. Oh. Well. Never mind.

The article was about a researcher from the University of Oregon who was looking for physiological factors to explain the 8 percent of sheep who are gay. I say who cares why it happens, how fabulous are those sweaters? The researcher postulated, as scientists are wont to do, that the mechanism in gay sheep might have human implications. That set the PETA people to worrying, blogging, and gang e-mailing that the science would lead to breeding out homosexuality.

If that were true, the Bush "administration" would already have made a Manhattan Project out of it. Or at least a Chelsea Project. Go ahead. Research away. Need more money? Better equipment? Are you sure that microscope is big enough? How about an institute? No need to fill out those tiresome grant application forms. Here, use this stem-cell money we have lying around.

Whenever I have a big reaction to something trivial, it is usually a sign that there is a stinging nettle of truth nearby. At times I do think we are more sheepish than gay. While I honor the importance of separatist spaces for occasional rejuvenation, we have made very safe little pens for ourselves. We bathe in the sheep dip of conformity. Mind you, it is not a strictly homosexual trait. We mirror the mainstream

herd. For seven years the Bush "administration" has used the invisible fencing of fear, cattle prods of intimidation, and nipping dogs of war to cull the herd of nonconformists. The national shame of Guantánamo is a quotidian reminder that our government can make anyone disappear. We have all been lulled into thinking that we can create "safe spaces" of homeland security for ourselves.

And gay sheepishness is real. It comes from gay shame. Despite progress, gayness still carries an ick factor, a yuck and eew we internalize inchoately. So we learn early to try to be the best little gay girls and boys so that we will not get beaten up. We carry that people-pleasing into adulthood. In my own writing and performing, I experience it as a pall of self-censorship. I go for the groan of the easy pun, the obvious physical trait joke—he's so wooden, he's so old—or the cheap shot. Luckily I have careful editors, courageous friends, and a fiercely critical girlfriend who push me to think deeper, make more connections, name names, call out racism, and then, of course, make it funny.

········································································

# Just Rehab Those Slurs Away!

### March 2007

Brrrrrrrrrring! Brrrrrrrrrrring!

Another late-night drop-off to a Gay Slur Rehab located at a secure, undisclosed location somewhere in the frozen tundra of northern Minnesota. Open 24/7, slur rehabs are proliferating faster than nonbinding resolutions—and not a minute too soon.

Owing to security concerns, the location of the Gay Slur Rehab is known only to the directors of GLSEN and GLAAD. Persistent rumors place it right across the street from the top-secret unit where they housed Mark Foley and Reverend Ted "absolutely heterosexual" Haggard.

An admissions counselor, who requested anonymity because of the incredible stupidity of his job, said it has been very busy lately. "We've had Tim H., Isaiah W., Michael R., Mel G., and, briefly, Ann C. here. They were all treated and released. Joe B. was treated on an outpatient basis on our N Campus, during Articulate, Bright, Clean, Good-Looking Black History Month. Tonight we admitted the head of the Joint Chiefs of Staff, Peter P."

PR train wreck and verbal bed-wetter Tim Hardaway arrived at bleep-away camp, speaking in voices, alternately belligerent and sorrowful. He spoke first in his own voice: "You know, I hate gay people." But then, eerily, he seemed to channel Maya Angelou: "I am committed to examining my attitudes."

After an initial "faggot" outburst, *Grey's Anatomy* star Isaiah Washington hardly spoke at all. W. successfully avoided lockup the first time he came out with the *f* word at the office. Only when the "intense" actor slipped and threw f-bomb number two was it time for gayhab.

While the methods of W.'s attitude adjustment rehabilitation are shrouded in mystery, we do know he successfully completed the program. He was released into the community service program, where he will donate a free performance on *Dante's Cove* and allow gay designers to pin fabrics on him on *Project Runway*.

Ann C. was a hopeless case, not because her homophobia was untreatable but because it was misdiagnosed. While trace elements of homophobia were found in her small, cold veins, a counselor, who requested anonymity because it was so mortifying to work there, said, "For her, bigotry is just good business. Truthfully? I don't think she believes half the crap she says." Although court-of-public-opinion-ordered, C. was not admitted to the facility, because she arrived with seventeen camera crews to document her anonymous treatment. Other patients had to wear their slur rehab hoodies low just to get to their midmorning session, "How to Get the Mea Back in Your Mea Culpas."

The presiding counselor, who requested anonymity because of his own sexual orientation, said, "Peter P.'s case poses real challenges. He has no real remorse for his statement and in fact feels victimized for his deeply held opinion of the immorality of homosexuality." In a

radio interview, General P., who oversees the daily conduct of an immoral five-year-old war, had opined that homosexuality is immoral, much like adultery.

"Adultery! Which we can't do because we can't get married either," added his fuming caseworker, who requested anonymity because he had been the partner of the presiding counselor for years.

In a separate news item, it was announced late this morning that General Pace has been nominated for the Golden Slurry for "Gay Activist of the Year." "It's early in the year, but we haven't seen gay people this organized since Anita Bryant tried to get gay teachers tossed out of Florida public schools," said the owner of a highly profitable chain of Florida slur rehabs, who nonetheless asked to remain anonymous because of the high rate of recidivism in his programs.

Gayhab is obviously just the latest twist in the slur rehabilitation biz. Everybody is so tetchy; a whole *Sesame Street* alphabet of offense is available for rehabbing. The *n* word, the *f* word, the *q* word. (Not queer—quagmire.) There's gold in them there swills! Mel Gibson is developing a Malibu campus for his Jewish Slur and Chemical Dependency Unit. Michael Richards has been looking for investors for his N-Word B-Gone Unfunny Farm franchise, but so far no takers (although with his tendency to flounce around in fat-black-woman, soft-bigotry body suits, Eddie Murphy is starting to look like a possible partner). Tyler Perry denied being approached by Richards.

But, hey, this field is wide open. Now that *saying* something mean gets you in more trouble than *doing* something mean does, I recommend we model future slur rehab regimens on the Sarah Silverman Program. You will be able to say any old horrible thing you want. If you say it innocently enough while wearing a two-toned cotton baseball shirt, you will create a post-PC, guilty-pleasure persona that is babelicious, witty, and winning. Say it funny, as if you do not really mean it, and you will never again have to meet with the man from GLAAD or even GLSEN in a small dark-paneled rehab room.

# Edible Equality

## May 2007

It is dinner season! Instead of proms, we gay people have dinners, and I for one cannot get enough, uh, I guess that is chicken. Yes! It *is* chicken! Often the dinners are in the same hotels as the proms of the younger (than ever) people from local high schools. It always makes for a lovely, amusing mix in the lobby. Even the tuxedos seem confused.

In Boston, I had the great good pleasure of emceeing the Sixteenth Annual Fenway Women's Dinner. Not to brag, but I am the Ryan Seacrest of the LGBT dinner party circuit. For more than thirty-five years, Fenway Community Health has worked to improve the physical and mental health of the LGBT community in New England. The Fenway proudly focuses on the needs of the underserved, especially women of color and those living with HIV/AIDS. They are *Our Bodies, Ourselves* embodied, and the research they do not only has transformed LGBT health care but also serves as a model for health care worldwide. Many of the yearly honorees are astounding practitioners: Dr. Susan Love, a pioneer in women's health and breast cancer, and Byllye Avery, the founder of the National Black Women's Health Project.

The Westin Copley was awash with lovely ladies in black cocktail dresses and gorgeous tuxedoed variations making a racket in the silent auction area. Boston's Mayor Menino, with a perfect attendance record for Fenway fetes, was in a feisty mood about the legislature and the holdouts on the gay-marriage initiative. The new governor of Massachusetts, Deval Patrick, was present, saying the right things with neither notes nor hesitation. He mentioned that his wife was complaining that they had to leave and would miss the dancing after. He promised next year they would stay to dance and celebrate. When they left, Diane's dance card was preemptively full up.

In Atlanta, I emceed the Twentieth Annual Human Rights Campaign Dinner. I am an *amuse bouche*. Winston Johnson, a longtime, legendary Atlanta activist, reminded me that I had been at the first Atlanta dinner. He also teased me that back then I had made a dildo joke even though Coretta Scott King was in attendance. I confess I got carried away. But when I apologized to her after, she looked me right in the eye and said, "Don't be silly. I've been around."

Twenty years ago I met Representative John Lewis. As a young man he had been chairman of the Student Non-Violent Coordinating Committee (SNCC) and had been severely beaten for all the world to see during the 1965 Selma-to-Montgomery march. He was humble yet ferocious then, and he is that and more now. He was at the dinner. Those twenty years of dinners represent Atlanta's and the South's shared struggle for civil rights.

At dessert we all bit, and turns out the trademark blue-and-yellow HRC equal signs were edible! While that equal sign is a brilliant bit of branding, I have always wished that for a few years we had gone with a better-than sign. Nonetheless, we all feasted on equality.

A girl needs a rest between dinners, and I took my R&R with the Oliviettes at a huge sprawling Club Med in the Dominican Republic. From a formal black crepe suit one night to a sarong and SPF 45 the next day! It is a wonder I do not just split down the middle. Since we comics are generally never in the same city performing at the same time, one of the best parts about "working" an Olivia cruise or land-based vacation is getting to catch up with my sista comedy gal pals. I love to see them perform. In answer to your unasked question, "Are they funny offstage?": yes, they are hilarious and spontaneous. Despite jet lag! They make me howl. On that trip I hung out with Michele "Next to the Last Comic Standing" Balan; Karen Williams; René Hicks, who ably used and defused the "nappy-headed ho" uproar; and Miss Victrola Shaw, who once again allowed me to apprentice with her on the Oldywed/Newlywed Game.

Next stop on the dinner circuit was the National Center for Lesbian Rights bash in San Francisco, celebrating its thirty years of work. Under Cirque du Soliel–ish trapeze acts, towers of amps and Jumbo-Trons, three thousand celebrants jammed the Fort Mason Center, a former military base perched by the white-capped San Francisco Bay. Onstage, as I surveyed my joyous lesbian San Fransisters doing their

interpretation of the gay male circuit party, I remembered that early *Well of Loneliness* warning so many of us got subliminally or overtly. We would be lonely and alone, sad spinsters darning socks next to the hearth, dependent on the grudging hospitality of an older brother.

Later I heard that the cocktail dresses were edible.

····························································································

# Incoming!

## June 2007

Psssst! I cannot tell you what I had to do to get it, but I finally secured the secret formula for the Gay Bomb! And just in time for Gay Pride Month! Okay, I will tell. It involved a bunch of tequila and a recent visit with some fly-girls from the air force's Wright Laboratory in Dayton, Ohio. That is all the freedom of information you are getting.

Apparently the military has a program to develop nonlethal weapons: e.g., megaton tasers, stare-downs from Mr. Karen Hughes, whatnot. Nonlethal weapons are so thoughtful, if a tad late for thousands of Iraqis. The air force requested $7.5 million from the Pentagon to develop a so-called Gay Bomb, which would release a chemical aphrodisiac to turn enemy forces gay, causing them to become more interested in sex with one another than in fighting.

Unfortunately, I was unable to obtain the formula, also proposed at the time by the air force, to make bees angry enough to attack enemy forces. It was not clear if those attacks would come while the enemy lovers were having sex. Which is just plain mean. As you know, the Air Force Academy is located near Utah, the Beehive (not hair) State. There must have been concern that the bees would flee their collapsed colonies, illegally migrate across borders, and attack some yummy Mormon sister-wives.

The Gay Bomb proposal, per usual, has nothing to do with women. Because it takes a bit more than an incoming canister of eau de Tom Ford, a soupçon of Rufus Wainwright qua Judy Garland, and some

K elixir to flip straight women soldiers into lesbians. Hint: If you leaflet U.S. women with promises to pay their full student loans, faster than you can say "Private Benjamin" you will have a lean, mean fighting lezbeen machine. Turns out everyone loves multipocketed camo pants.

News of the Gay Bomb surfaced back in 2004 and has resurfaced in tandem with the renewed political need for a gay wedge (aka get-out-the-base-vote) issue. Tired old "don't ask, don't tell" is the new gay marriage. It is so 2004. And so desperate.

The tide might be turning. Under the carpet bombing of "I Love Paris in the Slammer" coverage, defense secretary Robert Gates announced that the contract for General Peter "Homosexuality is immoral" Pace would not be renewed, though he could still pitch for the Yankees. In our house, we believe that Paris Hilton works for Karl Rove.

Military recruitment goals are not being met. Five rabidly Catholic Supreme Men who never served in a war ruled that pregnant women must deliver children (aka soldiers) even if it is a threat to their health or it is against their doctor's counsel. It is a perfect storm of a long war. Would somebody ask Dick "Grandpa" Cheney where I can find some aluminum tubes for my Gay Bombs? I will need some rainbow decals too. I want to lob one into Congress. Then the Supreme Court. Not the White House. Maybe Pierre, South Dakota.

## The Month Formerly Known as June

### June 2007

It is Gay Pride Month in New York City, and I do not know if it is a result of that premature spring-ahead clock-change thing that George did to save energy, but it seems awfully early this year. That is why it

has been suggested that we just call it Gay Pride Era, claim the century, and be done with it.

One of the traditional kickoffs of the week's festivities here in New York is the mayor declaring that he is no longer a Republican. Or at least that is a new and cherished tradition. We hope every Republican mayor follows Mike Bloomberg's lead. And the New York legislature got the gay marriage bill out of committee. It only took thirty years to pass a gay rights bill in New York, but we remain optimistic. What is our option?

The other tradition of N.Y. Pride is the LGBT Center's Annual Garden Party. This year was #24 and was held again on one of the Chelsea piers. I had the honor of emceeing for the eighteenth time. My Staten Island posse, under the direction of my promo domo, Michele Karlsberg, was out in full force, getting names for the mailing list, handing out fliers for upcoming shows, finding all the free stuff, and just being their usual fun schmooze-operator selves.

I love our New York center. It truly is the gay heart of Manhattan. Everyone loves it, so it is jammed to the rafters. It is time to expand. The $50 million capital campaign got a boost from Manhattan borough president Scott Stringer's $1 million pledge and the $8 million pledge from council Speaker Christine Quinn, our favorite Irish-American lesbian. The grants were announced at the Garden Party and were a lovely testament to Richard Burns, the center's executive director, and his twenty years at his job.

It was a gorgeous night. We watched the sun set over New Jersey. We heard great entertainment—two-time Tony Award winner Tonya Pinkins, recording stars Chris Garneau and Kirsten Price, perennial favorite Lavender Light Gospel Choir, and a hilarious impromptu set from Michele Balan, last seen on *Last Comic Standing*. And because the GP24 was subtitled "A Taste of Pride," the food was a smorgasbord of New York's best, a dim sum of the divine. The people were proud and well fed.

June 23, the night before the big Sunday gay pride march, is the Dyke March. The chant at the first Dyke March I attended was the lovely and welcoming "We're dykes, don't touch us, we'll hurt you." It is difficult to be a lesbian and a people-pleaser, so the chant gave me pause, but I was hoarse from yelling it by the time we got to Washing-

ton Square Park. I have found the chant helpful in lots of situations. When I am unable to get customer assistance in one of those big-box depot stores, I just start the chant. Generally before I can get to "we'll hurt you," someone in a vest is there to help me.

I cannot wait for the march. It kicks off at five p.m. from Bryant Park, and we don't even get no stinkin' permit. That's what I'm talking about. So-called organizers wear T-shirts emblazoned with "Unpermitted." We just march, dammit. Well, not really march. It is really more of a mingle. It is a sea of ex-lovers. And lesbian moms. And lesbian cheerleaders. A few signs: FEMMES AGAINST FASCISM. And my favorite moment is when the young girls start peeling off their tank tops and climbing the streetlight poles. I do not know who gives the signal, but this year I am fixing to find out. And then I am just going to give the secret signal in every city I visit. Happy LGBT Pride Era!

........................................................................

# Friends of Bill and Dorothy
## August 2007

At the last Palm Springs golf classic I attended, I saw two drunken lesbians duking it out in a parking lot puddle. At one of my shows, a woman was so blasted she thought I was speaking directly to her and actually stood up to answer a question I thought I had posed rhetorically. Club Med now includes drink prices in its vacation package. By 10 a.m. Tuesday, "All you can drink" has become "Drink all you can." In the middle of a posh fundraiser, I realized that the lovely gay male donor with whom I was chatting was completely smashed and had already left the building.

Recent studies have found that alcoholism affects 30 percent of the gay population, compared with 10 percent of heterosexuals. Thanks to Britney, Lindsay, and other fully loaded wild girls, the gap may be narrowing. Almost one third of lesbians and gay men are addicted

to drugs. It is not that homosexuality causes addiction, or addiction would just be a gay problem.

We live in a country fueled by alcohol and drugs. What we witnessed after Hurricane Katrina was not just a natural disaster but a whole area of the country going through an unplanned detox at an involuntary rehab. The president is a death-denying dry drunk who once deliriously and mistakenly described Dick Cheney as "a half-glass-full kind of guy." No telling what Laura is on. For her sake, I hope it is something strong.

Now I can assure you, I am no angel. I played in a lesbian softball league, not for the love of the game but for the after-beer. Ditto golf. If you had one bottle of wine with friends at dinner, why not eight? I would still be smoking pot if I could find things on my computer. I came up in a lesbian culture that had chem-free seating areas. I thought it was quaint, probably good for those who *really* needed it, but not for me.

Nor am I Carrie Nation, that old temperance babe of the early 1900s who perfected an antisaloon direct action she called "hatchetations," the envy of any ACT UPper. The only good thing that came out of Prohibition was Mafia movies and eventually *The Sopranos*. (Cut to black.)

And I do not mean to bite the hand that gave us Zima. Years ago, when Absolut-ly no one was funding gay anything, liquor companies saw a niche and poured it on. Gay leaders, desperate to keep their doors open, agonized over being taken on by liquor companies. I do not ascribe malicious intent, but as I walk through the last stumbling, mumbling partiers at the end of gay prides, I think of the Russian czars keeping the peasants pacified with cheap vodka.

I'm not trying to make you go to rehab. No, no, no. That is way too much eyeliner for me. The next few years of gay liberation require our consciousness. As we win freedom a day at a time, I promise it is going to be a real high. Have a six-dollar bottle of Pride water instead. Have the one with bubbles.

# ENDA, Don't MENDA

## October 2007

On a scale of one to Betty White, the Ellen DeGeneres Iggy custody story, unlike the off-the-charts Michael Vick dogfight gambling story, is about a seven. And this is not just me talking. The home office has run the story through a rigorous, impartial sampling process that included the Mitt Romney "Irish setter in the dog carrier on top of the family car going on a ten-hour ride to the family vacation" story. They have been very thorough. The needle on the meter never even brushed eight.

Thanks to YouTube, I caught up on Ellen's story. When I first heard about the dogfight, the cynical me wondered if it was sweeps week. This despite the fact that I have been treating my cynomalaise with drugs and hot rocks massage. On day #3 of the saga, Ellen delivered a deftly impassioned call for acceptance and forgiveness and a let's-move-on opening monologue. She mentioned the death threats and violence toward the Mutts and Moms Dog Rescue Shelter and said flatly, "It's not okay."

Ellen's reasoned plea for everyone to sit and stay could be a blue-print for warring factions everywhere. Condoleezza Rice, who is do-ing the traditional end-of-term desperate diplomatic shuttling for a Mideast solution, might have learned a thing or two. I hope Condi has TiVo.

Watching the intensity of the first day, when Ellen broke down, I marveled that she had shared none of this intense emotion when she came out, lost her sitcom, and surely struggled with the consequences of coming out. But that is a lot to ask and really none of my beeswax.

And, full disclosure: I am not a dog person. When I was three, a big German shepherd jumped in my stroller and scared the bejesus out of me. A year later I saw a boxer tear another dog's ear off in a dusty, adrenalized swirl in my otherwise placid neighborhood. Dogs

know I am not a dog person, and each one tries to prove that she is not like those other dogs.

For the last few months I have been advocating that the genuine outrage that dog lovers and the people who love them evince in these stories should be harnessed for other events that people do not seem to care about at all. I tried to get Nancy Pelosi to use "Puppies don't have health care" to override W.'s veto of the State Children's Health Insurance Program.

Ironically, while this Iggy top story rules the week, in Washington, D.C., LGBTs are trying to pass ENDA, the Employment Non-Discrimination Act. Or actually they are trying *not* to pass ENDA. How weird is that? The bill had languished around for years under the slobbying efforts of HRC, but suddenly gained a new leash on life when Representative Barney Frank tried to get it out of committee, minus the provision for ending discrimination against our Ts, transsexuals. And why now? I bet you can get ENDA with a T when W. is gone.

On a scale of one to Renée Richards, it is not okay.

Three hundred and two organizations have signed an endorsement to reintroduce transsexual protection to the bill. Wisconsin's fearless representative Tammy Baldwin motioned to put trans protection back in the bill.

It is a wicked mess. How about "Labradoodles need rights too!"?

....................................................................................

# Power Is Sexy! Action Is Hot!

## February 2008

Those were the popping, unapologetic mantras of the recent National Conference on LGBT Equality, sponsored by the Task Force in good old Detroit, Michigan. Formerly known as the National Gay and Lesbian Task Force, the grassroots organization stopped trying to accom-

modate all the L's, G's, B's, T's, and Q's in their name and downsized. They are not concealing their LGBT identity. They are a force and they get tasks done. Good thing the action at the confab was hot, because otherwise it was fa-reezing. Not that I ever found my way out of the Escher-like hotel for four days.

The night before the conference, I performed in Ann Arbor. If you are a performer on the road in Michigan, you have to book a show at the Ark in Ann Arbor. Started in the mid-1960s by a consortium of four local churches as a coffeehouse and teach-in location for students, the Ark still self-describes as "dedicated to the enrichment of the human spirit since 1965." For the last forty years it has been run by Dave and Linda Siglin, but throughout its history the Ark has depended on volunteers, and it is still a vital core of the progressive community of southern Michigan. It was like a liberal bends chamber on my way to the rarefied radical atmosphere of the "Creating Change" conference in the Motor City.

It was the Task Force's twentieth activist conference, and it was like old homo week. I saw a lot of old pals—the brilliant historian and biographer of Bayard Rustin, John D'Emilio; the longtime activist and founder of Southerners on New Ground (SONG), Mandy Carter; and the conference cofounder and general hell-raiser, Sue Hyde.

The old homos embraced me, and I them. My peers once changed the health system to deal and deliver around the AIDS crisis and thus transformed U.S. health care. It has since devolved to a single-prayer plan: "Oh, please, God, don't let me get sick." But my comrades are at it again, bringing their skill sets to transforming aging in this country. We are having a second wind, so watch out.

Trans activists, who have always been welcome at the Task Force, were fierce, funny, and firm with me, making sure that I got the T in every mention of our community in my duties as emcee of the daily plenary sessions. Then we talked fashion.

And, happily, I fell under the spell of roving gangs of young gay activists who took me to poetry slams, dances, and real-time organizing. We fought about Clinton vs. Obama, kissed, made up, and pledged to work to defeat whatever old warhead the Republicans threw up. At least half of the young gay activists are gainfully employed in LGBT organizations at the local, state, and national levels. What used to be

an unpaid, volunteer passion that you surreptitiously requisitioned into your day job or went to after the paid day's work was done is now a bona fide career move! They are smart, strategic, media-savvy, and delightfully entitled. We are in good hands. I would feel fine retiring. But I won't. Two words: George Burns.

We heard Julian Bond of the NAACP. As we waited together backstage, Bond told me that he uses lots of my lines. He said the first time he uses the line, he credits me by name. The second time, he credits "a friend." He said, "By the third time, it's mine." It was a high compliment. Bishop Gene Robinson of New Hampshire addressed the gathering with unsurprising fiery feminism. He really is the Gay Gene. At the last plenary of the conference, the longtime civil rights activist, music historian, and full-throated singer Bernice Johnson Reagon and her no-musical-genre-is-safe-around-her daughter Toshi Reagon performed and sent everyone off, inspired and fired up for the work of creating change.

If you feel a subtle or seismic shift in the energy of your LGBT community, some hot, powerful, sexy LGBT activists have returned home from the Task Force "Creating Change" conference, and they are already kicking it up.

........................................................................

# Go, Golden Staters! Go, Buckeyes!

### May 2008

Four years after San Francisco mayor Gavin Newsom's gay marriage block party got shut down by a very testy legislature, the California Supreme Court lifted the ban on gay marriage statewide. Woo-hoo! Make some noise! Tie strings of tin cans on injustice's gas-guzzling bumper as it lumbers out of town.

Of course, some Grumpy Guses are already throwing rice pudding. Do they have day jobs? They reject the California court's two

bedrock arguments: that tradition alone does not justify discrimination, and that sexual orientation must be part of the strict scrutiny in equal protection. Be prepared to smell that "choice" chestnut roasted again on the flames of hate.

But before the end of civilization as we know it—and really, is that such a bad thing?—or the anti-gay-marriage people get their store-bought signatures certified for another ballot initiative, let's pop some corks! Hip, hip, bye-bye to hypocrisy!

While our behemoth national cruise ship flounders and stalls, the little tugboats of states are working the harbor, hard-hauling and nudging a national course correction.

I was just in Columbus, Ohio, to do a show the night before the third annual Lobby Days, sponsored by a group called Equality Ohio. Three hundred and sixty activists from all over the state spent money on gas, got child care, and took time off work to converge on the Ohio state capitol to urge their legislators and representatives to pass a Senate and House bill to end antigay discrimination in housing and employment.

After Equality Ohio's well-organized session on the how-to's of lobbying, ordinary Ohioans, proud of their Buckeye home, walked out of the Hyatt function room and across the street to the statehouse to tell the stories, big and small, of the impact of discrimination on their civic and personal lives. Their laser focus on the job at hand was an inspiration.

Truth to tell, I have been bumming a bit through the long sexist, racist slog of the national primaries, so I am happy to dust off my party hat, put on my pretty party dress and combat boots, and whoop it up.

Thanks to the California plaintiffs and to the good citizen lobbyists of Ohio! And to the other forty-eight states where the grind of working for justice is done every day! Go, Buckeyes! Go, Golden Staters! Lead the way! Woo-hoo!

## The Perfect Heterostorm

### May 2008

Every Sunday, before I check the newlywed pictures in the *New York Times* Style section, I like to see if I know anyone in the society pages. Thank goodness I know the philanthropist Aggie Gund. She is my friend's mom, and she always helps my totals. Years before the *Times* officially started posting same-sex couple pix, I would pore over the pictures with my gaydar magnifier and pounce: "Hoo-ee, look at these two! Now that is a gay marriage!"

Despite their policy of same-sex inclusiveness, there is still some Sunday fun. The same-old-sex couples still lean into each other like Siamese twins attached at the soft spot. With a plumb line and simple chalking, I have documented some same-sex couples rejecting the *American Gothic* pose, tilting slightly toward each other by about three degrees. I am still trying to prove my theory that there are more degrees of separation in the same-sex pictures during election cycles.

After the same-sex marriage photos began appearing in the *Times,* I noticed that more photos of older, nonwhite, and mixed-race couples began appearing. Although they too followed the guideline that straight people must be photographed conjoined at the fontanelle, it was a subtle change.

After painstakingly recording my calibrations in a small black notebook, I scan the "Vows" highlight story. I used to call friends and do dramatic readings in various accents, with hilarious commentary, but they have asked me to stop. My girlfriend will not hear it.

Then I scan the "Modern Love" column for its revealing straight-people slice of life. Recently I read the heartbreaking hetero trope of intern-leaves-supportive-partner-after-attaining-medical-degree. But it was about two women. I actually knew the jilted. Thus proving my mother's suspicion that there are not many lesbians and I know all of them.

Now, I do not know if the *Times* plans these things—I should query that very helpful ombudsman—but that "Modern Love" story oddly foreshadowed the big *NYT Magazine* cover story the next week: "The Newlywed Gays! Life among young men who are married [to men] in Massachusetts could not be more normal. Strange."

The cover featured a stylized homo-normativity scene, complete with suburban McCrèche and guys who all looked like Pee-wee Herman, with a manic touch of Jack from *Will and Grace*.

Because features about lesbians are generally ponderous stories about lineage—more "Who's the father?" than "Who's your daddy?"—and someone always ends up in tears, the author focused on young gay men. Besides, he himself was an embed in the life.

The author followed the lives of several young white married and engaged male couples to find out why they were marrying. Because they can, seemed to be his answer. Unlike the older generation of gay men, young gay men who can come out much earlier in life and experience age-appropriate adolescent mayhem have the will and grace to settle down sooner. Paul Reubens might have not gotten so mekka-lekka high if Jambi had urged patient temperance, gay marriage is a-comin'!

At the same time this heavily anecdotal article appeared, a study of young gays and lesbians in New York City revealed that 92 percent of females and 82 percent of males expect to be partnered in a monogamous relationship after age thirty. Fifty-five percent of females and 67 percent of males thought they would likely raise children. One can conclude that fewer women want children because they actually know what is involved.

On the eve of the fortieth anniversary of the Stonewall riots, how are things in Gothamora? I do not want to get all Gail Sheehy on you, but at forty, the gay movement seems to have gone through its stormy adolescent passage and is finally ready to settle down, get married, and have kids.

So I would rather get all Kübler-Ross on you. Instead of a midlife passage, the gay movement might be in the fifth and final stage. We have been through denying we are gay; fighting angrily with church and state about it; bargaining about military service, marriage, transgender inclusion; being depressed about constant ballot initiatives,

setbacks, and roadblocks to full citizenship. The movement is in a "can't beat 'em, join 'em" stage five of acceptance.

It makes me sad.

Then it doesn't. I have lived in sin for twenty years with a Hindu, who, though proclaiming her secularist street cred, has a deep belief in reincarnation. Do not even try to swat a greenhead fly around her. She just keeps coming back to her radical activism. It has rubbed off on me. I hope that in the ashes of the acceptance are the seeds of a new liberation movement and that new pictures will appear. Not only lucky, white, happy gay men but also poor lesbians, people of color, and older people.

..................................................................................

# He Sees Gay People

### June 2008

After my Memorial Day run at the Crown and Anchor in Ptown, I took a lovely local nine-seater Cape Air plane into Boston for the twenty-seventh annual Massachusetts Bill of Rights dinner. The pilot was in training and kept reading the laminated instructions list. It was a quaint reminder of early flight.

But if you want to meet some real risk-takers, look no further than the honorees at the ACLU dinner. The founder of Boston's Wainwright Bank, committed to progressive lending and minority ideals, disproves the real current mantra, "When banks compete, you lose." While Errol Morris's film *Standard Operating Procedure* is certainly not what you would call a date movie, Morris deserved the recognition for telling the back-story of Abu Ghraib. Ironically, on the day of the release of Scott McClellan's belated tell-all book *What Happened*, Watergate's John Dean was honored for his work. I asked him to please thank his son, Howard, for his good job rebuilding the Democratic Party.

Mass. ACLU also honored the twenty years of work of their legislative director, Norma Shapiro. The diminutive Jewish grandmother strong-armed the Catholic boys of the legislature into passing gay marriage in Massachusetts. Talk about a vein of iron. Lots of attendees got me aside and whispered, "She knows where the bodies are buried." I bet she knows the whereabouts of fugitive Whitey Bulger.

And then it was off to San Fransisters and the National Center for Lesbian Rights Gala Dinner. And more about gay marriage They were partying and celebrating the lifting of the ban on gay marriage in California before they go off to fight yet another costly ballot initiative. I wondered why we cannot sue the fundamentalists for harassment. The NCLR lawyers told me they could not, nor can they initiate a ballot to get rid of ballot initiatives. Dang.

Two of the marriage plaintiffs, my good friends Jeanne Rizzo and Pali Cooper, took me to a Giants game at their lovely in-town stadium. It was "Until There's a Cure Night" at the park, and the SF Gay Men's Chorus did a mini-concert before the game. The crowd cheered them and longtime city pol and comic Tom Ammiano, who read a declaration from Mayor Gavin Newsom. We have come a long way since 1981. The Giants lost in extra innings, but we were long gone, because it was a gusty forty-two degrees, and I did not have on my stadium hot pants.

I kicked off Gay Pride Month by appearing in the True Colors Tour lineup at Radio City Music Hall with the Cliks, the Indigo Girls, Regina Spektor, Rosie O'Donnell, the B-52s, and, finally, Cyndi Lauper, still kicking her eight-octave range. I pinch myself.

After the craziness of California—and I must say, there was some flaunting and taunting: "So when are you and yours coming out here to get married?"—it was great to be back in New York, where Governor David Paterson issued an executive order that New York State must recognize out-of-state same-sex marriages. After Governor Spitzer and Paterson's own revelations about his marital excursions, it might be that New York does not actually recognize in-state same-old-sex marriages.

Nonetheless, it was a proud moment. Paterson said that when he was little, whenever his parents went out, they would leave him with his uncles, Stanley and Ronald. They played cards with him and

helped him with his homework. Because of that early and formative familiarity, the governor's startlingly simple and fair directive made me proud of my deep New York roots. Though legally blind, he sees gay people.

# Citizen Arrests

Bush checks off the remaining items on his bucket list. Work on the Bush Liebrary, check. Appearance on *Deal or No Deal*, check. Drilling in ANWR and EVERYWR, check. "My bad" is not on the list. When God speaks directly through you, you cannot make mistakes. The Bush years were like being in a horrible relationship. On the first date, someone slipped us a roofie. We find it hard to explain why we were with him. Everyone who "didn't want to say anything" is yammering at us. We have a wicked hangover. No need to try to remember the events of our long last night. That will come. Hopefully, it will involve several appearances before the International War Crimes Tribunal. We fight the lassitude from post-Bush traumatic stress disorder. The one true thing we learned during the Bush regime is that one person can change the world. Now is the time. Get busy.

# Third Term

## April 2006

I was worried. I had started to identify with George Bush.

When my partner and I were arguing, and it was not going well for my side, I would say, "May I remind you we are at war." After she implied that I had gone to some idiotic non-sequitorial school, I would pause and point out, "And now you are giving comfort to the enemy." I would promise to do things and then just go out and do whatever I damn well pleased.

I found it unsettling how much George and I were alike. After all, we both have a vague grasp of geography and history. "Wow, Brazil is big!" he said when Brazil's president showed him a map. George and I both have definite workout goals, though I do not have to close down the state parks in Maryland to ride my bike. We both hate to admit we are wrong—especially after we have declared the mission accomplished and we're off to be greeted as liberators.

This annoying affinity was not some late outbreak of compassionate conservatism. It was not brought on by fevers from the avian flu caused by all the Democratic chickenshits out there (Russ Feingold excepted). For the next Senate Judiciary Committee hearings, we should install big windmills in front of Joe "I'm throwing my hair in the ring" Biden's mouth. He could heat the Northeast in the dead of winter.

It was not March Madness or remnants of Winter Olympics fever. It was the Stockholm syndrome—the behavior of hostage victims, who over time become sympathetic to their captors. Five years of being detained by the cartoon in chief and his trigger-happy toon pals can do that to a girl.

You will be happy to know that a recent Republican strategery conference snapped me out of it. I have taken off my beret and put away my Uzi. At the conference, Bill "ask your doctor" Frist and Mitt

"full of s——t" Romney and others all speechified before prospective donors. What did the crowd want to hear about? The economy, torture, the war? Aren't you sweet.

No, the war party wanted to hear about the sacredness of life. Clue: Recruitment is falling short; the war is running long. The Support the Troops ribbons are starting to look like infinity symbols. They are going to need every body they can get. And there they go again—marriage is "between one man and one woman," a bee-otch slap to Mormon Mitt from Sam Brownback.

Sometimes I like to think the red of the red states stands for embarrassment that a majority of them voted for George. The blue of the blue states stands for them holding their breath, waiting for the other side to implode. News flash: The rabid are not thinking "my bad"; they are thinking "third term." They never bothered with that pesky Constitution before. Why start now? Why else is George always mentioned in approval rating polls with John "Karl's next project" McCain and Hillary "the hawk" Clinton?

Ken Mehlman, head of the Republican National Committee, and I believe, son of Larry "Bud" Mehlman, said that Hillary Clinton has a lot of anger. You want anger? I'll give you anger. George Bush, I wish I could quit you!

## Peace of My Mind

### October 2006

Republicans have rolled out their midterm election strategery: free Viagra for everyone! Kidding. But they are having a hard time getting it up and keeping it up. When Bush, Cheney, or Rumsfeld labels the opposition "appeasers" and "fascists," I hear a very grown-up voice in my head sing-songing, "I know you are, but what am I?"

The Democrats seem incoherent, perhaps suffering from one too

many earnest let's-get-religion, we-need-new-values language fo-
cus groups. And pathetic. If I had Mission Impossible/Abu Ghraib/
Katrina footage, I believe I could make a clear statement. I would not
even have to use the talking-with-your-mouth full, inappropriate-
massage footage of President Potty Mouth in Europe. Perhaps I am
naive. The Republicans seem dipped in Astroglide. Nothing sticks to
them.

And I do not doubt that that unindicted tube-squeezer Karl Rove,
so "brilliant" that he brought his boss to a 36 percent approval rating,
was behind the national distraction of John Karr, who was arrested in
Bangkok after his false e-mail confession to the murder of JonBenet
Ramsey. Check the ship's log for an earlier Karl Rove visit to Thai-
land. As election day nears, watch for the reappearance of O.J., the
Lindbergh baby, and something Tom Cruise. When they drag out that
tired old wedge issue of gay marriage, you know they got nuthin'.

Welcome to the insane swirl that is my brain on national politics.
The resident activist in my house has taught me that taking action is
the only way to interrupt despair. I do not mean buying one of those
Countdown to Bush's Last Day hope-ometers. Besides, I would not
put it past them to declare martial law and a third term. That Consti-
tution has been nothing but an inconvenience. Again the swirl.

But it is possible to stop the swirl of despair, especially if you go
local.

My older brother Bill and his wife, Mary, live outside Philadel-
phia. Yes, that makes him Bill Clinton, but not that Bill Clinton. (I
also have a sister named Monica. Another time.) They both felt frus-
trated and heartbroken by national politics and wanted to *do* some-
thing. Although, or because, their district is heavily Republican, Bill
decided to run as a Democrat for their local town council. For months
he knocked on doors and talked with his diehard Republican neigh-
bors. After they ranted about the other Bill Clinton, they vented about
George Bush and Rick Santorum. My brother argued that they should
channel their anger into a vote for him. His victory was one of the
most cheering, proud moments I have had in a long time.

In Provincetown this summer I began to notice rainbow flags on
guesthouses, businesses, private homes. I assumed they were the tra-
ditional gay flags, but then I noticed the white block letters PEACE

over the rainbow stripes. Each day I noticed more and more flags. One night I biked by a simple candlelight vigil on the post office steps and found the seller of the flags.

Tracey Primavera, a New York City transplant, is a massage therapist and has been active in Ptown's antiwar group, which has held a vigil in front of Town Hall every Saturday for five and a half years. She said she wanted more; she wanted to be for something. Each night she sold flags to locals and to vacationers from all over the world. She said being pro-peace offered more of an opening than being antiwar. With each sale or no-sale, conversation happened.

Interrupt your version of swirl. Get involved in electoral politics and speak out for peace. Knock on some doors. Hang out your rainbow peace flag.

........................................................................................

# The UN Goes to Junior High
### November 2006

I could hardly get to the computer repair shop. My system crash had occurred as I wrote about UN Security Council meetings this fall in Manhattan. The town was a gridlocked parking lot. When I finally arrived, the computer guy told me, "Your logic board is broken." "Of course it is," I responded. "You should see what I'm writing." The raw data I have been inputting would shut down any logic board.

The UN had morphed into a middle-school playground at recess. There was bullying. George Bush was talking directly to the Afghan people, as if they had electricity and were watching him on their flat-panel TVs. There was the "I know you are, but what am I?" taunting from Bush's fellow traveler, Iran's president, Mahmoud Ahmadinejad. There was name-calling from Hugo Chávez. The onlooking crowd of delegates did "Oh no you ditn't" neck moves that needed no translation. Unfortunately, some of these boys have nuclear sticks and stones.

Perhaps it is the lingering sulfurous futility of trying to make something logical out of war that has so twisted our times.

In his efforts to open religious dialogue, the pope said that Islam is evil and inhuman. Now come on over for some beer and a brat! Who is his press person? Someone from Tom Cruise's old entourage? I tried the papal "apologia" in confession: "Bless me father, I'm sorry you think I've sinned." I was asked to leave.

In response to the selectively released intelligence study which stated that our presence in Iraq is worsening the situation there, that master of illogic, Dick Cheney, said we must stay in Iraq because the situation is worsening.

In dizzying daily conversation, those who have changed their position on the war think they deserve more street cred than those who were against it from the start.

What to do in the face of such paralyzingly deliberate, denying illogic? In addition to the bracing necessary acts of civic participation—working for a candidate, registering voters, running for office, voting, fundraising, manning phone banks, monitoring polls—I humbly suggest another tactic.

The sit-in was a simple, brilliant tactic of the civil rights movement. The die-in was a brilliant tactic of the AIDS movement. To those esteemed protest methods I would add the laugh-in. Not that too-short-lived variety show from the Nixon years, though it is still quite subversive, even in reruns. No, the laugh-in maneuver I am talking about can be done in large groups or one-on-one. So far this hidden weapon cannot be detected by the new behavior detection officers on security.

After listening to huge steaming piles of illogic for a respectful five minutes or so, let go with a guffawing, rip-snorting howl of bend-at-the-waist laughter. If you have infiltrated a crowd, at a lecture or rally, let out your whoop, pound on the seat in front of you, recover yourself, then, perhaps with a small wave of the hand, indicate to those around you that you have regained your composure. Wait ten minutes and do it again.

If it is a one-on-one situation or a small dinner party, as you right yourself after your hoot, wipe your eyes, try to catch your breath, sigh, look at the speaker, do a respectable double-take, and wide-eye the

person with "Oh my God, you *mean* it." Repeat. They will never say those things again with any degree of confidence. It is a sure no-fire way to interrupt illogic.

................................................................................

# I Don't Heart Huckabee

### December 2007

For my high school graduation, I asked for and received a doctor's supervised diet. After the weigh-in and the weekly shot of "vitamins," my doctor, who was later disbarred for amphetamine abuse, gave me a thought for the week. One week his homily was about the flames of hell. He told me that they burned very verily hot because of all the fat.

People have a grudging respect for Bush because he has been able to maintain his weight for seven years. That's all he has been able to maintain. Remember all the hooting at the pictures of Bill Clinton in his jogging shorts? Now that he has a perfect body mass index, he is internationally beloved.

Primary voters can say what they want, but the reason they like Huckabee is that he lost one hundred pounds. You can never be too thin or too insane. On foreign and economic policy he is a lightweight, but the spirit of a fat guy is still in him. Not Santa. No. Jerry Falwell might have blowed up real good and died, but his ideas are alive and well in the Reverend Huckabee.

Forget the homophobia once removed of the debate on gay marriage. The rev goes right for the gays. Though it pains him to say it, he must say that homosexuality is an aberrant, unnatural, and sinful lifestyle. He has been dragging out that claptrap about love the sinner, hate the sin. And do not kid yourself, he hates them both, the sinner and the sin. For him, quarantining people with HIV is not a matter of homophobia. It is a matter of public health and safety. Do not do me any favors, former fat boy.

One undecided voter in Iowa said that Huckabee lost her vote when he scoffed that there is no global warming in Iowa. She said they used to have snow, now they just have ice storms. Her business, Bees of Iowa, has been harmed by global warming.

Although I am a proud secular fundamentalist and radical pluralist, tonight before I go to sleep, I'm going to eat two Twinkies and pray for a Huckabee colony collapse.

# Happy International Women's Day!
## March 2007

And three cheers to the national Concerned Women for America for putting out a press release defending Ann Coulter, claiming that she had said "bag it," not "faggot." Yes, that is right, John Edwards is a big ole bag it. They did not specify paper or plastic.

Methinks Girl Gone Wild Coultermania has Karl Rove all over it. Hey, one woman's conspiracy theory is another man's history. While cable heads debate 24/7 curtailing the use of the f-bomb and the n-bomb, without a mention of free speech, our eyes are turned from I. Lewis Libby and the more inconvenient truth about death-defying Dick Cheney. I, Kate Clinton, say it is no coinkydink. I want Libby to do his time in Gitmo. I want him to have the same habeas corpus delicti as those detainees. He would look great in an orange onesie.

Or perhaps the I. Scoot could exchange it for a candy-striper onesie and do some community service at Walter Reed Hospital? Talk about *Notes on a Scandal*. (Sidebar: I just wanted to say to Judi Dench, "Judi, Judi, Judi, watch Cybill Shepherd on *The L Word*; see how it's done.")

Support the troops, indeed.

What were we thinking? After WMD lies, Katrina "rebuilding," Mission Accomplished—that the VA was being run right? Heckuva job, Surgio, heckuva job. I used to whine that these last months of

Bush felt like the longest of my life, but they are nothing compared to the hospital time that our dear wounded veterans are enduring. For them, the yellow Support the Troop ribbons really are infinity symbols.

Bush and Cheney give new meaning to the Year of the Pig. They keep giving us completely extraordinary renditions of the world. This International Women's Day I am having a big bonfire with the obscene number of Bush-bashing books I have bought over the years. You know what porcine pair I would like to put on a spit over the pit in a lulu of a luau. Enough. I am making room on my shelves for the post-Bush stories we all better be ready to write.

. . . . . . . . . . . . . . . . . . . . . . . . . . . . . . . . . . . . . . . . . . . . . . . . . . . . . . . . . . . . . . . . . . . . . . . . .

# DC 911

### April 2007

Quick! Is the line "No one does a better job of not doing their job better" a description of the Bush "administration" or an ad for *Reno 911*? What's the matter? Having a hard time with the image of Karl Rove in tight, tight state trooper short shorts? Or Harriet Miers, pointing her Glock and squawking, "Fire 'em all"? Or Alberto Gonzales, who always looks like he is laughing at us behind his mirrored trooper sunglasses, snarling, "I serve at the pleasure of the president."

If you guessed *Reno 911*, you would be right, but there was that nanosec of doubt, wasn't there?

Comedy Central's hilarious updated version of the Keystone Kops actually seems competent by comparison with the Bush administration. The private firm that was hired by the feds to erect the seven-hundred-mile border fence was recently busted for using illegal immigrant workers. If I were in charge, I would build a sixteen-lane highway along the border with lots of on and off ramps. On patrol, I'd be wearing knee-length multipocketed shorts, driving a Prius, and

dragging Lou Dobbs. Could we just put the fence around the White House?

If the presidential election were held tomorrow, we would save a lot of money. The first-quarter results of the big obscene presidential money race are in, and if you combine the amount the Democrats and Republicans have extorted, we could pay off a year of student loans for everyone, start to rebuild the Katrina-ravaged South, and still have some cash left over for that big victory celebration Bush and Cheney are planning in Iraq.

The election is nineteen months away and the whole thing sounds like some tiresome fantasy sport race. Let me know when it is over. The Bush legacy is cleanup on aisle 5. After eight years of the mess, everybody has to work.

I have dibs on a job already. Whirled traveler incurious George was dropped into Machu Picchu for the international version of a *So You Think You Can Dance?* contest and was airlifted out after ten minutes. He had no idea where he had been. After the heli-dust had settled, locals called in esteemed shamans to sage the place and get out the bad spirits.

My job is organizing a public spectacle. It is very informal and it is driving my professional activist girlfriend crazy. "Do you have permits? You have to print up leaflets informing people of the purpose and facts of your protest. You'd better reserve a block of hotel rooms. What about Porto-Johns?" I tell her she is confusing codependency with spontaneity. We shall see.

I have contacted all my woo-woo gal pals, some psychically, bundled up the necessary herbs, and written a ritual modeled on the recent saging of Machu Picchu. Through expert use of viral marketing, on January 19, at six p.m., the night before the inauguration, we are gathering at the Ellipse and then we are going to surround the White House. We will fire up our sage bundles and smoke out the bad spirits. Yes, you can bring Lysol spray, but we are trying to go green.

We call it Macho P.U. We serve at the displeasure of the president. Be there or be square.

......................................................................

# Buzzkill

### April 2007

Albert Einstein—and he is one Alberto we can believe—once said that if the bees disappeared, mankind would have only four years of life left. As you know, I am hoping that colony collapse disorder (CCD) will turn out to be an urban legend, like that one about the counter-clockwise toilet flow south of the equator. I think what we are really witnessing is the collapse of the white male colony. As predicted, it is not pretty.

The Supreme Court's 5–4 decision in *Gonzales v. Carhart* to support the ban on partial birth abortion partially paralyzed me. Judge Anthony Kennedy, a man who recently judged a mock trial of Hamlet, a disturbed young man with a sword, not a Glock, fancies himself quite the writer, and wrote floridly for that damnable 5–4 majority. Next up: honor killings.

Justice Kennedy said that the main argument against late-term abortion is that women will have regret. Perhaps Kennedy was working out some problems he has been having at home with a regretful woman. Perhaps his wife did not get her bid on a pear-shaped finial she wanted on eBay and was horrible to live with for weeks. You know how we get when we are regretful. He is not going to put up with that again. In a codependent crisis moment, he decides it is the man's job to protect the little ladies from our emotions around abortion, so he will not have to cop to the fact that he is the one who cannot deal.

And I can blather like this because it has been the Festival of Amateur Analysis Week, from Dr. Sean Hannity to Tucker "with a T" Carlson to good grief counselor Paula Zahn.

Of course I am reviewing my memories of the excitement I felt at Kennedy's lofty writing in our favor, in the *Lawrence v. Kansas* case, decriminalizing sodomy and overturning *Bowers v. Hardwick*. Has Kennedy changed? Could it have been all the henpecking from that

regretful woman at home? More piling on of the amateur analysis. Don Anus must have been relieved this week that the spotlight was off him. That whole sorry episode killed Don Ho.

And thank goodness that empty-headed, incompetent cronyism is confined to the workings of the Justice Department. It is, isn't it? Again I review my memories of other hearings—Watergate, Iran-contra, Anita Hill, Guantánamo (no, wait, did we even have one?)—and I have never seen more evidence of white male colony collapse. Perhaps the ban on abortions, combined with abstinence-only sex education, is the new army recruiting plan. Brilliant! It is going to be a long war.

Gonzales is the hapless tool at Justice who makes you almost long for the good old days of Ashcroft. Republicans are worried about voter fraud. That there is not enough of it. Gonzales was called before the Senate committee to answer questions about the possibility of a politically motivated firing of eight federal prosecutors. The Gonzales hearing was no *Mind of Mensa Show*. He remembered nothing. It was like Reagan, the Iran-contra years. George W. gave him a "heckuva job" performance review. If I premember correctly, Alberto will be gone next week.

·············································································

## Lights Out on Bush

### May 2007

In the early 1970s, when I did my first semester of practice teaching in Oneonta, New York, I rented a room from a recently widowed older woman whose big rambling house was a few blocks from the high school. Mrs. Chase was a gradualist and did not agree with the spring ahead/fall behind clock change, so she informed me that she would change her clocks ten minutes a day for six days. She had a lot of clocks. By the third day of her rotation, she started missing a cuckoo

clock here, a grandfather clock there. I was late for Thursday home-room duty.

Despite my own gradualism, my body adjusted grudgingly to this year's premature spring forward, mandated by the 2005 Energy Policy Act, but my resentment seethes unabated. Supposedly the capricious change saves energy. I think it is just so George can take his evening dirt-bike ride earlier in the year. Wearing a helmet for no apparent reason. What does he protect with that helmet? Any energy saved is more than offset by the fourteen-car motorcade which takes him to and from the Maryland park closed to the public for his private ghost ride.

We are a nation addicted to oil, said the pusher. Bush is now a born-again evergreen, transfixed by all the things that can be trans-formed into ethanol. But he still gasps when he tries to say global warming.

At a hearing in March, Democrat Henry Waxman of California called as a witness Philip Cooney, who served as Bush's chief of staff at the White House Council on Environmental Quality. Cooney, who is not a scientist, took up editing instead. In 2003 he blotted out the following sentence, which the government's own scientists had writ-ten: "The 1990s are likely to have been the warmest decade in the past 1,000 years for the Northern Hemisphere." And he added: "The Earth's climate has changed dramatically throughout history and will con-tinue to change due to natural variability." Cooney, who now works for ExxonMobil, testified that he was trying "to align these communica-tions with the Administration's stated policy" on global warming.

When an ice shelf the size of Manhattan snapped off his mother, George finally took some notice, but officials choked again and blamed it on El Niño, which is Spanish for George Bush.

Here is an idea for saving energy. If we all burned the shelves of anti-Bush books we have, I am estimating we would have the equiva-lent of a year's supply of fuel.

Perhaps we could harness the hot air blown from the Democrats on the topic of withdrawal. I am told that under the proper pressure per square foot, chickenshit makes a lovely high-octane reduction.

As annoying as the spring forward has been, the fall back might not prove so jarring. It used to be the last weekend in October. Now it is the first weekend in November. The Twizzler lobby is huge, and they

worked hard to save another hour of daylight for Halloween trick-or-treating. Like the oil companies, the dentists' and orthodontists' lobby has to be happy for the expanded drilling.

While it would be wonderful to have an extra hour of sleep so that we can all be well rested for the November elections, I recommend for 2008 that we extend our meager daylight savings to the second weekend in November to optimize all available light for poll watching.

## Curb Your Mitt!

### July 2007

It is a known fact that there is nothing more difficult than trying to do political organizing in a resort town. You call for an evening meeting and the response ranges from "And miss the sunset?" to "Sorry, low tide, goin' clamming." In that spirit, it is hard to get oneself, i.e. me, organized to answer the blog gotta-make-the-doughnuts imperative. Especially when the daylilies are giving it their orange alert all one day at a time. I just do not want to miss it.

Dear blog reader, stuck at your computer, I am sure you are hearing blah blog blah, the dog ate my homework. But then, speaking of dogs, along comes Mitt Romney, and I practically broke a nail getting to the keyboard. Seems the terminally handsome Mormon (that is two *m*'s) was driving the family to a summer vacay and the car was packed to the gills. The gills are a new fuel-economy thing. The family dog was apparently treated as a Monty Python after-dinner mint. Mitt could not possibly fit it in the car.

So Mitt, who is making a bid to be chief caregiver of our nation, had the bright idea to put the beloved Irish setter in a car tote and put the tote on top of the car for the ten-hour ride. Neither the dog nor Mitt was wearing an astronaut diaper. The terrified dog got car sick, or it could have been unrecalled dog food from a certain large, soon-to-be-Olympic-host country. Mitt's best friend let go a stream of dog

poop so voluminous, they had to pull over to a car wash, hose down, and resume their trip. The dog was still up top.

The story has been in the local Cape Cod papers, and I can tell you that Mitt has lost the dog-owner vote. The incident has even cut into the man-on-dog sex homophobe theorist vote. The car wash bloc is also a bit swayed. The story does not have as many comedy possibilities as Old Number Two shooting his friend in the face, but good enough on a slow summer news day.

It is circuit party week here in Ptown, when guys from all over the country come to town to party on down for four days. The testosterone levels have totally canceled out the estro-swarm of Memorial Day weekend, when all the young college girl grads from all over the Northeast come to town. But I swear to God, I think I saw Vlad and George drive George's dad's cigarette boat up to the pier and hop on the all-night orgy party boat before it left for a night of carousing on the very high seas. I will let you know what I find out.

I am off to help the talented people at my summer place of employ—the Crown and Anchor—get our float ready for the Independence Day parade. Each summer we have a Codependency Float. There is nothing on it. We pull it ourselves. And en route we ask caring questions of parade watchers. "Do you need a sweater? You look cold. Here, take my sweater. No, take my sweater. " Maybe this summer we will wear Codepends and ask Mitt to join us. Once a gland marshal, always a gland marshal. Don't forget to pack the dog.

# Hypocrites Galore

## September 2007

A disturbing disorder is sweeping the nation. First there was SAD, social anxiety disorder. Formerly known as "shy," SAD is fear or apprehension regarding social situations. Then there was an epidemic of

RLS, restless leg syndrome, not to be confused with the twitching next to you on the delayed N.Y. to D.C. USAir shuttle. Now there is SHF, sexual hypocrisy fatigue, and I have a wicked case of it.

Plain old hypocrisy fatigue I can handle. Harriet Miers, she who wanted be on the Supreme Court, showing contempt of court? Ho-hum. Alberto Gonzales, the nation's leading law enforcement officer, preemptively ordering the Justice Department not to prosecute contempt-of-Congress charges if they concern assertions of executive privilege? He wore me out with his hypocrisy long ago.

But after Ted Haggard and Mark Foley, I knew I was in the throes of a full-blown SHF attack. And when the story unfolded about David Vitter, I felt like a drowsy chaperone at yet another orgy. Yawn.

Back in the good old days of the Clinton impeachment, after the multiphilandering Newt Gingrich stepped down, his successor, the Speaker-elect, Bob Livingston, resigned when his extramarital affairs became public, thanks to the investigative hustle of Larry Flynt. Louisiana legislator Vitter campaigned for Livingston's vacant pedestal and won. During his campaign, Mrs. Vitter was asked what she would do if her husband cheated on her, and she said, "I'm a lot more like Lorena Bobbitt than Hillary. If he does something like that, I'm walking away with one thing, and it's not alimony, trust me." You go, girl!

Vitter is a family-values, antichoice, abstinence-only social conservative who called for Clinton to resign to "preserve the moral fabric of the country." He led the election-year fight to bring the Marriage Protection Amendment to the Senate floor. He smarmed, "I don't believe there's any issue that's more important than this one." Ah, but there was: how phone logs work.

The still-hustling Larry Flynt notified Vitter's office that the senator's number had appeared several times in the phone logs of a D.C. escort service. From an undisclosed location, perhaps on a tryst with the no-show Harriet Miers, Vitter e-pologized for the very serious sin of his past, took responsibility, and said that he had received forgiveness from his God and his wife. Apparently Lorena Vitter's vitriol has a cutoff date. No word yet on whether Giuliani has dropped Vitter as his southern regional campaign manager.

During his prayerful seclusion, more allegations from other prostitutes surfaced, challenging that single "sin" statement. Salacious ru-

mors of a diaper fetish—Pampers, not astronaut—whipped through the Internet. You can be sure Joe Lieberman, the Senate swinger, did not start them. He needs Vitter to stay. After a week in which he worked on his press victimization 'tude, Vitter held a press conference, flanked by his wife, Wendy, ably played by Allison Janney, C.J., the press secretary on *West Wing*. And then he was back to work.

Despite all the dizzying, juicy details, my *schaden* has lost its *freude*. Like erectile dysfunction (I guess), I just cannot get it up anymore for the predictable disconnect between screed and deed. Blow jobs pale in this seven-year snow job, and I will take orgasm over wargasm any day. Give them all a per diem.

......................................................................................................

# Precollision Intelligence

## October 2007

On long flights, I like to watch movies with the sound off. When I get home, I watch with the sound on and compare the actual story with the story I have made up. I was so wrong about *About a Boy*. I hope they never show *Snakes on a Plane* on a plane.

I also like to watch muted ads to try to figure out what product is being shilled. Whenever I see an actor friend in a commercial, I have a clue, because she claims she specializes in the lower gastrointestinal tract. So that does not count.

During the World Series (note to Red Sox: when you sober up, do not even think of hiring A-Rod—he is a spoiled, troublemaking diva), between the interconnected beer and erectile dysfunction ads, I laughed every time that woman jogger ran into the parked car. Even when she got up, dusted herself off, and slammed into the car again, I laughed. I still do not know if the ad is for running shoes or Lasik surgery, but my girlfriend is shocked at my low threshold for the pain of others. I thought I knew what the unsettling "precollision intelligence" ad was about, but it actually has something to do with a car.

Full disclosure: I suffer from the condition known as precollision intelligence, and I wish there were a pill for it. It would have to be the size of a satellite dish. When I have forced myself to watch the train wreck that is the president do a press conference, I have kept the sound off. He seems to have a little pal planted in the front row that he smirks at, like "Can you believe they're fallin' for this crap again? Whooee!"

First, is it my imagination or is my own presidential profiling accurate in assessing that the mysterious hair area 51 between the presidential brows is growing? The area, on others known as the "third eye," has a thatch of hair that now melds into his eyebrows, making for a unibrow that looks like a very wooly caterpillar. It is going to be a long nuclear winter.

Let's review: when we have weapons of mass destruction, they are called nuclear weapons; when other countries have nuclear weapons, they are called weapons of mass destruction. Everybody has caught on to the discrepancy. Ahmadinejad, Chávez, Putin, even Castro's brother are laughing in our faces. We have become the Rodney Dangerfield of countries.

As the Republican candidates sink further into a swamp preowned by the Democrats and now in foreclosure, my precollision intelligence tells me that while boy George jaw-jaw-jaws about working with other countries to spread democracy, he is fixing to bomb Iran, declare both a state of emergency and a third term. My friends think I am being paranoid, but watch for the developing silly-gism of: Katrina is to California just as Iraq is to Iran. Do not just watch their lips move. Unmute. "California shows how much we learned from our mistakes in Katrina [especially if we are rescuing white people]. We've learned so much from our mistakes in Iraq. We're ready for Iran."

He declared a first term and nobody stopped him. You tell me, why not a third?

...........................................................................

# Bush as Belichick
## January 2008

In his first presidential summer, with the Crawford split-rail, photo-op fence behind him, George Bush, the science guy, squinted into the sun and announced his Just Say No to embryonic cells in stem-cell research. It was kind of lame.

In fall 2001, he was forced to take off his lab coat and put on his bombardier jacket to deal with terror cells, not stem cells.

Now, owing to the enormous progress in Iraq (i.e., everyone has fled or is dead), our favorite political scientist has donned his white coat and wraparound safety glasses again and claims responsibility for the latest discovery in cell technology.

Picture a young Frankenbush surrounded by bubbling, billowing beakers in his secure lab down in Nixon's old bowling alley. With his trusty Mr. Wizard chemistry set, he adds four pluripotent genes. Eureka! Thanks to him, instead of using human embryo cells, researchers can now use cells from human skin, especially if the skin is straight, white, and Republican. Researchers are already prospecting around plastic surgery sites in Palm Springs.

In Colorado, this discovery will free up the embryos needed for the embryonic personhood ballot initiative just approved by the state supreme court there. The arduous task of going door-to-door collecting thousands of signatures means they are going to need more blastocyte boots on the ground.

The *New York Times,* made an inch and a half narrower to cut costs and yet still wide enough to carry Dowd, Brooks, and Kristol columns, reported and seemed to believe that the president had modest goals for his last year in office. I heard that snort. What? You think they are going to attack Iran? Apparently you did not read David Brooks's assurance: "The Bush Administration is not going to attack Iran. Trust me." That "trust me" thrust me into a frantic search for my passport. It has not expired. I have pages left.

The Bush policy of unintended consequences has taught us one thing: one person can change the world. In just seven excruciatingly long years, Bush's arrogance has destroyed the United States as the last remaining superpower. It is okay. I was never comfortable with all that unseemly, messianic, imperial chest-thumping.

When you are a haughty, unbeaten number one, everyone resents you.

It is a lot of pressure, and you become like Bill Belichick and the New England Patriots. Spying on other teams, getting caught and denying it, piling on, running up the score, taunting, glowering monosyllabically at press conferences, and wearing whatever old cut-off hoodie you want.

Bush and his buddies have greased the skids of our decline and finally lost one for the Gipper. Guantánamo and torture made our national symbol the American spread-eagle. Welcome to Post-America. When not slightly heartbroken, I am oddly relieved.

......................................................

# PBTSD

### March 2008

The pope is coming to Manhattan and we do not have congestion pricing. It is going to be hell.

I cannot focus on the news, but near as I can figure, the Widow Ratzinger is carrying an Olympic torch for Cardinal Egan of the Diocese of New York. He's come a-courtin'! *Antiques Roadshow* says it is the original torch! Benny the Dict will be saying a mass at St. Patrick's Cathedral and one at Yankee Stadium. It could cause a new curse of the Giambino on Yankee pennant chances. Cardinal Egan will throw out the first host.

Though I used to be a conscientious Designated Bush Watcher, these days I watch the news distractedly. I do not think I am alone. The *New York Times* has accommodated by becoming news CliffsNotes.

I am dissociative. I pretend that HBO's *John Adams* is the breaking news. I went to the very helpful WhatTheHellIsWrongwithMe Web site and self-diagnosed what ails me. I believe I have early-onset PBTSD, post-Bush traumatic stress disorder.

My presenting symptoms of lethargy, distraction, and dissociation are compounded by Clinton fatigue. And I am one. What *is* Hillary Clinton's sleep number? I am tired for her. But why does she have to have an exit strategy and Petraeus does not?

I have a wicked case of Oblahblahma cynicism, which prevents me from seeing the magic of another guy with little experience, known for his talking skills, good or bad. He has already weenied out with his timetable babble when questioning Petraeus.

But with my PBTSD, I would not know a revolution of the human spirit if I fell over one. No, I can't. I cannot stomach another story of pathetic boomer parents bonding with their darling children by taking cooking classes, snowboarding, and switching from Clinton to Obama. Yet another reason not to have children.

With a preexisting condition of precollision intelligence, I have profound disbelief that the disaster that is John McCain is an actual presidential contender. Two words: George Bush. How can Republicans say that they will vote their pocketbook, which has been so thoroughly picked?

At night I am plagued by rational fears that Condi Rice is going to spring fully formed as a vice-presidential running mate out of the giant wen on McCain's cheek. Condi has been giving signals that McCain has not been picking up—there is a great start. McCain's wife, Republican Spice, has been scrambling them and will snap Condi's neck if she gets an inch closer.

Instead of going to therapy, I have been watching HBO's *In Treatment*, with Gabriel Byrne and my favorite, Dianne Wiest. Not really. I cannot watch. I am too restless, but my friends who watch say the therapist never discusses insurance coverage, copay, or prescription prices. Or that hour sessions are fifty minutes long.

# The Unconflicted White Man

### March 2008

My Indian girlfriend makes me capture crickets using a humane catch-and-release program that would make a Lou Dobbs Minuteman Border Patrol pitch an epi. I go quickly to the door and, at a decent distance from the house, release the critter into the wild. I can be driven to violence by night sounds, but when it comes to crickets, I bow to my skittish, delegative partner's wishes. I honor her loosely held belief in reincarnation.

One morning while reading the paper, she announced, as if I had asked, that she finally knew her preferred form of reincarnation. Still drowsy from my night patrol, and frowsy from trying to make sense of Maureen Dowd, I asked, "And?" As if she were declaring a Halloween outfit, she stated that she wanted to come back as an unconflicted white man. The "straight" was understood.

While my fallen-away Catholic beliefs still imbue my eschatological hopes for an afterlife, I have totally embraced her tenet. Not George Tenet. Though he is a perfect example of a UWM. In the midst of endless war, UWM are perfectly at peace with themselves. Wideawake from cricket racket, I think, "He must have some regret for what he has done." It is pure projection on my part.

The UWM roster grows each day. Donald Rumsfeld, who claims that he is now "out of the loop" on the war, wants to start an institute to encourage more civic participation in government. In the *Vanity Fair* issue that finally chronicles the media goring of Al Gore, gung-ho war ho, Christopher Hitchens chronicled not his war makeover but his spa treatment. Karl Rove angles to captain the Swift Boat Veterans Threatened by Powerful Women, aka the Giuliani campaign. Dick Cheney continues in his role as head of the executive plus legislative-executive branch of government.

In China, when officials err, they have the decency to kill themselves. In the United States, they go on victory-lap book tours. The

press rollout of UWM Alan Greenspan's preemptive save-facebook could serve as a model for a coordinated, well-executed exit strategy. Like a bad penny, Greenspan was everywhere—*Newsweek, Jon Stewart, The News Hour*. On *60 Minutes*, he Cheshired as the blindingly blond embedded reporter Leslie Stahl dimpled, "You were a jazz player?" The underreported party spoiler was Naomi Klein's simultaneously released *Shock Doctrine*, as welcome in the discourse as an unclaimed backpack in a bus terminal. If I Did It v. You *Know* You Did It.

The grand master of UWM, If-I-Didiot in Chief, announced in a recent legacy-building interview that when he leaves office, he wants to start a Freedom Institute. "In other words, people can come to the institute and talk about freedom." His tight tautologies make Miss Teen South Carolina's ramblings sound sane. Mostly he noticed from his father and Bill Clinton that you can make big bucks speechifying. Such as. "Gotta fill up the coffers, y' know?"

Southern Methodist University is resisting housing the Bush Presidential Liebrary. I think they should put the Bush Shelf at the Creation Museum. Nestle it into one of the "Six C's of Creation" dioramas. It would fit perfectly in "Corruption and Catastrophe." Rapture Man is divinely unconflicted because he has done his job as independent contractor of precollision Intelligent Design. The landing strip for the second coming is ready. His work here is done. He is the one in whom only he is well pleased.

# On the GLAAD Rag

## March 2008

One time early on in our beloved movement for full human rights, I was marching with the unsanctioned Irish gay contingent in the St. Patrick's Day parade and we were taking quite a hammering. The size and menace of the crowds closed in on us, narrowing our eight

abreast to nearly single file. As I marched my nice little Irish lesbian self past my people, an older woman screamed so forcefully, she blew her top dentures out of her mouth.

Time slowed. We both were united for a moment and watched her yellow teeth in their pink gums arc through the air, trailing a string of spittle. They landed and settled with a little joke teeth-chatter. We looked at each other in embarrassment. She resumed her scream. I resumed my march and stepped on her teeth as we continued.

The matter of the LBGT Irish contingent marching in the St. Patrick's Day parade is still unresolved. Our openly lesbian city council president, Christine Quinn, boycotted the march and instead was invited to march in Dublin's parade. My friend Kate Moira Ryan and I have a tradition. We don every piece of Irish knit clothing and every rainbow accessory we have, watch the parade on Fifth and Sixty-fourth for an hour, marvel at all the kids of color marching behind the Irish school banners, try to pick out all the gay people, then go eat Chinese. Each year over General Tso's chicken, she makes me tell my flying-teeth story. At this point I am not sure there was a little joke teeth-chatter. I did step on them.

Just as NYC was sobering up from the St. Patrick's Day parade, the big NYC GLAAD dinner was held at the midtown Marriott Marquis. It was a cuddly gay gridlock alert, color-code level rainbow. Despite a rollercoaster week of market, construction crane, Governor Spitzer up-then-down news, GLAAD fired up the JumboTrons, poured the sponsoring vodka, and put on a party.

There were stars aplenty, jammed corporate-sponsored tables; even the Tylenol PM–sponsored table seemed perky and primed for fun. There were pharma-fonted teleprompters and a dinner din that registered a ten on the can-you-hear-me-now scale. No, I can't, but your lips are gorgeous.

Allow me to report a few highlights.

*The Beebo Brinker Chronicles*, a dramatic compilation of the 1950s lesbian pulp novels of Ann Bannon, won a GLAAD Media Award in the "Most Fun Off-Broadway Lesbian Entertainment, *L Word* Eat Your Heart Out, Written by Kate Moira Ryan and Linda Chapman, Friends of Kate Clinton, And She Is as Proud as Can Be of Them, You Should Go See It, Tell Your Friends" category. I am not sure if that was the category, but yippee!

Despite the major comic red-meat temptations of Eliot Spitzer, the Jim McGreevy ménage à trois, and George W.'s market reassurances to the Economic Club as Bear Stearns collapsed a few blocks away, I had the serious task and honor of presenting the GLAAD Excellence in Media Award to Judy Shepard.

It has been ten years since Judy's son Matthew was brutally killed in Laramie, Wyoming, for being gay and out. Judy has been a tireless witness against antigay violence. Each new antigay atrocity is both a raw reminder to her of what happened to her son and a further spur to her activism. She graciously accepted the award and said she would of course rather have her son.

Her activism has impact. On the way out of the ballroom I ran into an old friend, who told me that after she had sent updates on her partner and three kids to her Catholic high school for her upcoming reunion booklet, she had been disinvited. Even though she had been class president and is one of the school's largest donors, she was not going to be issued a "Hello! My name is" tag.

Apparently she had been stewing in her juices about it until she attended the GLAAD dinner and heard Judy Shepard. She said that as she listened to Judy, she was texting the reunion committee and planning to use her own successful mainstream publicity company for a media campaign about her story.

That is what I call a successful dinner.

The original founding impetus of GLAAD was to be a media watchdog and to train the LGBT community in strategies to make media accountable for accurate portrayals of gay lives and issues. Perhaps as a victim of its own success, GLAAD has too often gotten away from its mission and gotten into grateful fawning over anything celebrity or vaguely pro-gay.

A friend of mine who sells airtime for a major network always reminds me that the competitive nature of dwindling major media markets makes the networks paranoid when they receive even the smallest of negative feedback. When I am whining about perceived slights, she stops me midwhine with "Did you call them?" It is something my girlfriend, a former public information director, aka propagandist, for the National Gay and Lesbian Task Force, has never forgotten.

We have all the major networks' comment-line phone numbers

on speed dial. Whenever we are watching some coverage, instead of just shrieking, she will excuse herself to go to the bathroom. I hear her leave a scathing message, a pause, then a flush, and she plumps back down on the couch with a satisfied smile. Try it. You will be glad you did.

........................................................................................

# Wii the People
## July 2008

In November 2006, just after those life-changing midterm elections, Nintendo, creator of Super Mario Bros., introduced an interactive game called Wii (pronounced "we"). The console was originally called Revolution, but Nintendo renamed it Wii because it was easier to pronounce in international markets and because Wii "sounds like it is for everyone," unlike Revolution, which would totally disrupt our sales, the game-making giant did not add.

A $200 million U.S. ad campaign—"Wii would like to play"—featured urban apartment dwellers, ranchers, grandparents, and parents with their children. In the United States, 9.5 million units were sold by May 2008. Worldwide, 50 million units are expected to be sold by March 2009. Queen Elizabeth II has played. Thus the royal Wii.

The most popular package is Wii Sports. Cancel that trainer and those gym fees! With the console hooked up to a television, players using a Wii remote can compete in simulated and simplified tennis, baseball, bowling, golf, and boxing. A player can create an avatar, or Mii (pronounced "me"). I am not clear what the Nunchuk attachment does, but it looks like an amazing vibrator. Weee!

Wii attracts casual, female, and elderly gamers, aka idled Hillary supporters. It is hours of fun, and popular in social gatherings. Karaoke machine makers are distraught. Families say it is a good bonding experience, and physical therapists use it for stroke victims and

injured soldiers. There are Wii tournaments and leagues. After some collateral plasma TV damage, straps holding the remote were made twice as thick. Overplaying has caused a tennis-elbow condition called Wii-itis.

It has been awfully hard to get sedentary Americans active, but they are breaking sweat with Wii! It has also been hard to get Americans engaged in the project of democracy, so I am plunking down $250 from my lovely stimulus check, buying a Wii, hacking into the console, customizing my own games, and then selling them on WiiBay.

*Wii voting.* Republicans are worried about voter fraud. Seems there is not enough of it. The game simulates the daunting task of gathering proper voting documentation: photo ID, driver's license with photo ID, passport, blood and stool samples, and getting a ride to a remote polling place. Gas money not included.

*Wii gay marriage.* Players assume gay identities, navigate competing, confusing state regulations, and plan a large wedding while fighting a statewide anti-gay-marriage ballot initiative. Gamer strategy suggestion: instead of having your bridal registry at Exxon, request that cash be sent to "No on 8," the National Center for Lesbian Rights' new PAC for marriage equality.

*Wii fatwa.* This game simulates a riot at the *New Yorker* headquarters. Avatars are based on the outraged Muslims who rioted when the Danish cartoons of the prophet were published. Players demonstrate and burn effigies of editor David Remnick until there is a retraction.

*Wii waterboarding.* One player chooses the puff-pastry features of Karl Rove. He defies subpoena after subpoena. Another player attempts an in-broad-daylight citizen's arrest of Karl while he is experting on Fox News. The Karlish player then tries to avoid waterboarding.

*Wii running of the banks.* Based on the running of the bulls, Wii players try to keep just ahead of bank closings, mortgage foreclosures, and predatory lenders. For extra fun, if players choose the game setting "Washington, D.C.," where the Supreme Court lifted the ban on handguns, players are allowed to turn on their loan officers.

*Wii Olympics.* Players are Olympics fans or competitors and must navigate the labyrinthine security system to get from their lodging to

their assigned stadium seats or starting blocks in time for the opening ceremonies. It can be modified for the free-speech holding pens at the summer political conventions. The game is recommended for business-level travelers only.

Also in the works: Wii eating—it really is hard to put food on your family. Wii armed combat—no, wait, those are already military training films. And a special collector's commemorative edition, a hybrid called Wii Grand Theft Election.

# Come On, Rogue

While my American family and our extended international family were whooping it up for the historic Obama victory, I banged pans and wept for joy with the best of them. But I also had that sad, dissociated, not-quite-part-of feeling I had at family gatherings when I was young. Actually, I have never felt gayer. Make no mistake: election night 2008 was an amazingly reparative night, a triumphant trifecta signaling the end of Nixon's southern strategy, the Reagan revolution, and the Bush regime. If Bush could consider his selection as president the first time and his slim election victory the second time to be mandates, then we can certainly call the Obama victory a landslide. It was a landslide, and it collaterally crushed us, as California, Arizona, Florida, and Arkansas passed antigay ballot initiatives. It was a bittersweet night. So excuse me if I seem an ungracious party-pooper, in danger of becoming more bitter than sweet. At this flabbergastingly amazing moment in our history, trust me, I do not like this feeling either. Action is always antidote to injustice. It is time for proactive strategies. If gay people are not full American citizens, let's stop paying taxes and reinvest in ourselves. It is time for our own ballot initiative to make divorce illegal and all divorced people disenfranchised felons. It is time for a general strike or rainbow flu. Until further notice, all gay people should go rogue.

# Project Runaway

### August 2008

A while back I was talking with my sister on the phone and told her the news that our niece was moving back east, and she practically hissed, "Fierce!" Then, to my confused silence, she explained, "That's Christian Siriano from *Project Runway.*"

Though my sister is a rabid anti-TV person, she is a passionate seamstress. Her guilty pleasure is *Project Runway.* She is now a Christian Sirianist. Of all the things I have done in my darling career, she was most impressed when I sent her a picture of the kindhearted taskmaster of the show, Tim Gunn, and me at a fundraiser. Desmond Tutu could not have gotten a bigger reaction.

Until this summer I had never seen *Project Runway.* At a lovely wedding dinner for two couples who had exchanged vows earlier that day, suddenly everyone was up and exiting before the cake was even rolled out to be cut. I asked the preternaturally hip fourteen-year-old son of one of the couples what the heck was going on. He gave me a look that made me feel even older than I did getting a texted VP announcement from Barack Obama and said, as he quickly exited, "Tonight is the drag queen challenge on *Project Runway.*"

Except for a few dazed straight people wandering the streets like some post-nuclear-family survivors, the streets of Ptown were deserted as I rode my bike home. The town had a personal stake in this *PR* episode. Two of our very own drag performers, Hedda Lettuce and Varla Jean Merman, were on the show.

Though I was not sure of *PR*'s format or point system or what accent Heidi Klum was doing, I was immediately hooked.

Thus far I have seen maybe four episodes, but from what I have seen, if the world does not end before the next presidential election, may I suggest we model our next national contest on *Project Runway*? Just as I am one of the last to know about *PR*, or to try on-

line banking, I am sure someone has already pitched this idea. It is so obvious.

Wouldn't you prefer a *PR* spinoff to the format we have now—endless primary campaign season, billions spent, Republican and Democratic circuit party conventions? It would be an eight-week season. Both parties would have four weeks to pick their contender, then four weeks for them to go up against each other. They would compete in individual and team competitions. The challenges would vary week to week.

To be read with a Heidi Klum accent:

This week you must work with a U.S. military and Iraqi civilian team to plan the withdrawal from Iraq by 2010. You will not be allowed to leave an occupying force or to send the troops home by way of Afghanistan.

This week you must design your own solution to our nation's health-care crisis. You will work with insurance companies and four people with chronic illnesses. Each can afford only $3 in copay.

This week you will work with the Army Corps of Engineers, the dreaded community organizers, and what is left of the infrastructure of New Orleans to draw up a plan for the restoration of the delta. You cannot rely on casino funding.

This week your assignment is to design a plan to reduce U.S. dependency on foreign oil by 50 percent in the next five years. You will be penalized for wearing fake hard hats and shrieking "Drill, baby, drill!"

Your final challenge, for the win, is to outline your plan to bring Dick Cheney and George Bush to trial before an international war crimes tribunal. You have two years to accomplish this.

You get the idea. Presidential candidates do not have to like the challenges; they just have to do them. We would get to see them in action as problem solvers, deciderators, managers, leaders, and not just

speechifying campaigners. Then we would all vote. I believe we have the technology to do it with our TV remotes. Press Select.

I am going to try to get this on the ballot in California as an election reform initiative.

........................................................................................

# Civic Tempura
## September 2008

My new performance-enhancement drug of choice is raspberry-flavored chewable Bonine for motion sickness. I am not a big ride-taker. The stationary horse on the merry-go-round is my personal Space Mountain. The lurching, stomach-churning political roller-coaster ride we call presidential politics has necessitated my self-medication.

Let's review. Barack Obama ran a brilliantly rolled-out ground war and beat Hillary Clinton in the endless Democratic primary. Hillary had a six-week air war planned, after which she would inevitably be greeted with open primary arms as our liberator. Didn't happen. She should have fired Mark Penn, her campaign director, earlier and given Bill a fist bump to the jaw.

The night the Obama nomination was certified official, McCain tried to steal his thunder by giving a flaccid speech before a backdrop with so much green tone he looked like a living yellow threat level. Steve Schmidt, grandson of Lee Atwater, son of Karl Rove, went postal and took over the campaign. The mission was to attack Obama the man as a thin empty suit, a celebrity, a joke. They ignored his policies.

The bruised and battered Dems did some mile-high healing at their convention, held in Denver a week after the Summer Olympics in China. Michelle Obama was first up on the balance beam—don't lose the black people, don't scare the white people. Marathoner Ted

Kennedy made it to that finishing line. High hurdler Hillary Clinton gave a gracious speech, no matter what Maureen Dowd might have heard. Bill Clinton did not unzip his pants, take out his baton, and gavel the convention to disorder as had been foretold. Joe Biden took the fiery torch from the Denver convention center to Invesco Field and expertly passed it to Barack Obama, who had ably captained the Redeem Team to primary victory. All of them nailed their landings.

The next day, as everyone sobered up, tried to find their clothes, to pack up and leave, John McCain lobbed the stink bomb of Sarah Palin into the detumescent room. Sarah who? A distant relative of Monty Python's Michael Palin? Sadly, no. This was Sarah, a body-checking, moose-gutting hockey mom, mother of five, NRA member, former Wasilla mayor, now governor of Alaska. She rode in on Hillary's girl-power high. It was a brilliant cry for help that put the focus on her, not on the train wreck that was John McCain.

Palin was the cynical choice of the Rove-Limbaugh Diaxis of Evil. She would guarantee the NRA vote, deliver the Vagina-American vote, and reenergize the right-wing religious base that had threatened not to vote for McCain but stay home and pray. I absolutely never believed the ruse that fundamentalists were in disarray, moribund, dispirited. They were just having one of their three-day waiting periods. When McCain rolled back the rock and the backwoods, backlit figure of Sarah Palin walked onto the stage, they were resurrected.

The 2008 Republican Convention in St. Paul was the 1992 Houston Convention redux, but with sixteen years more of vitriol. Gustav, the hurricane, a category 10 on the convenience scale, made it impossible for George Bush and Dick Cheney to appear and remind everyone of their Republicanitude. I believe they seeded the clouds. George sent his taped regrets. McCain and his devious minions made the first day of the convention into a Labor Day telethon for hurricane victims.

The convention resumed. To stoke the crowd, speakers used derision and mockery, generally the provenance of the professional comic like myself. Every speaker told the POW story of John McCain as if it had never been told before. The crowd cried as if they had never heard it before. The Hasselbackian Sarah Palin, feisty, femme, fast on her feet, and fertile as hell, gave a mean-girl, Lisa Lampanelli Friar's Club Roast of Barack Obama. After her roast, McCain, Sarah, and

her first-dude husband stood on the stage like Winkin', Blinkin', and Todd. Who cared what John McCain said?

The frivolous lipstick on a pig—or was it a pit bull?—phase of Operation Distraction died quickly with the serious rumblings of the collapse on Wall Street. The MSM tried to do their job for once and dig for information about the unknown quantity of Palin. They were accused of sexism by the born-for-the-first time GOP feminists. The Bridge to Nowhere story, the government plane sold on eBay story, the GOP version of Troopergate, were all debunked. Grainy You-Tubian videos of Palin anointed and exorcised at her local church were aired. Calls for her pastoral denunciation were not heard upon the land.

Palin was Velcroed to McCain's side for all appearances. Left on her wing-nut own in select interviews with Professor Charles Gibson, Sean Hannity, and Katie Couric, Palin appeared as unvetted and un-qualified for VP as Clarence Uncle Thomas for the Supreme Court. She was an empty business suit, a celebrity, a joke. Dan Quayle in a ponytail.

The problems on Wall Street went from pothole to sinkhole to gaping crater with steaming fissures of how-to-fix-it hot air blast-ing off manhole covers everywhere. What was bad for the economy proved good for Obama's poll numbers. That caused McCain to call for a suspension of his campaign, so that he could rush to D.C. for the first time in months to maverick the crisis. He must have taken a delay-plagued Acela, because it took him twenty-two hours to get from N.Y. to D.C.

I have thought of doubling my meds, but instead I will have what-ever Barack Obama is having. I really need an antidepressant the size of one of those blown manhole covers. Or perhaps I just need to move from the tiny island nation of New York City. I see every patently cynical brinkmanship move of the McCainiacs as the straw that will certainly doom his candidacy. This ought to do it, I think. Then I am told over and over that it was a brilliant, bold, fluid strategic move. We are battered and fried, a civic tempura. May I have the morphine drip now?

.........................................................................................

# Even Covergirls Get the Blues

## September 2008

Recently CoverGirl, the beauty industry giant, announced that it was hiring Ellen DeGeneres, beloved daytime talk-show host, to be the face of its next advertising campaign. Thankfully it was not the same week as the Lipstick on a Pig Festival. That would almost have been a bigger buzzkill than the Palin stink bomb lobbed into the Dems' Denver afterglow party.

A vice president of Procter & Gamble, the parent company of CoverGirl, said that while Ms. DeGeneres is an authentic beauty, she appeals to consumers who are "looking not so much for a role model as a woman they can relate to both physically and emotionally."

Ellen? As in the Ellen who challenged John McCain to walk her down the aisle, flashed her engagement rock, married her partner, Portia di Rossi, in a big summer wedding, and then shared her wedding album with her oohing-and-ahhing audience? She is now a role model women can relate to physically and emotionally? Let me apply my CG "Pinch Me Pink" blusher!

One industry observer said that Ellen's "sexual orientation notwithstanding," she is unlikely to alienate CG's demographic of seventeen-to-seventy-year-olds. CG must also be hoping for some crossover to the huge makeup-using drag queen market, but most queens use the really high-end stuff that does not parch your skin to a crème brulée crackle. Or a shattered glass ceiling. But seventeen-to-seventy is a huge demographic to be unalienated by lesbian orientation. Let me apply my CG "Shocked and Awed" lashblast mascara. It helps me not to blink.

What is really happening is that the sale of mass-market cosmetics is not withstanding the economic downturn. Sales plunged 6 percent in the first quarter of 2008. Yes, 6 percent used to be called a plunge. How quaint. Analysts say that in such a climate, brands try to retool

themselves to appeal to shoppers who prefer to see not a Britney or a Lindsay but a glamorously packaged version of themselves. But since when did all the ladies start honoring their inner soft butch? I look forward to seeing more tuxedo variants, sensible Fred Segal sneakers, and faux ties. Let me apply my CG "She's Just Like Me" lip gloss.

Cosmetics marketing consultants note that women, often disenfranchised in the cosmology of cosmetics, see an approachability in Ellen. They identify with her career ups and downs and appreciate her reinvention. With her approachability comes relevance. That certainly explains the mystery of Sarah Palin. I reapply my CG "Rosetta Stone" foundation.

Just as I held my breath waiting for the California wildfires to be blamed on gay marriage, I am holding my breath, waiting for Fuck Us on the Family's James Dobson's inevitable call for a national CoverGirlcott. He will say that the use of CG products causes lesbianism. That is certainly one way to get lesbians, who generally never touch the stuff, to buy CG products. The holidays are approaching. This season I am buying CG stocking stuffers for some of my favorite straight gal pals.

Fundamentalist women, and some men, deprived of their makeup are not a pretty sight. My own market survey shows so-called spiritual people often want this little piggy to go not to church but to market. Pat Robertson has a line of health products. I predict that they will introduce their own beauty line: Victoria Osteen's Secret teeth whitener, UnderArmageddon deodorant, and Rapture raspberry lip gloss.

Heck, if I knew how to do such things and had some start-up money lying around, I would brand the Rachel Maddow look. The new brainiac, lesbo-phenom commentator of MSNBC has been whupping old Larry King in their dueling time slots. Her unselfconscious, wonky downstyling drives my gay men friends crazy. "If I could just give her a pretty new chemise, she'd be fierce." Compared to the love-your-hair-hope-it-wins, bejeweled, cleavaged fancy newsgirls, Rachel's short-hair, no-necklaced neck, boi chest is a style self-described as assistant principal.

But if her ratings hold after the presidential election—and I, for one, am confident she can make the sausage-making of civic governance pretty and fascinating—I predict women on the street and on

the air will start scooping up soft butch, low-def jackets, forgoing all but the most basic of makeup, and letting the air out of their hair. Cannot wait to see Chris Matthews in Maddow drag.

.....................................................................................

# The Palin Effect

### October 2008

My head feels like the terrorists have won.

We went to a friend's house for dinner and the first presidential debate. My gal pal was quickly driven out of the TV room by McCain's smarmy opening gambit about Ted Kennedy's hospitalization. Unable to sit still, she nervously cleaned our friend's kitchen to a gleam it had not seen in years. Her Mrs. Clean efforts did not preclude periodic screams from the kitchen: "Do *not* agree with John McCain!" "Nail him now with the savings-and-loan scandal." "Interrupt Grandpa now!"

I TiVoed the debate and plan to play it when it is time for a thorough cleaning of our own kitchen.

I had thought of sending Obama a case of Red Bull for the next presidential debate. His personal serenity is highlighted by the desperate tics of John McCain, or, as we call him in our house, God Forbid. Obama's calm in the eye of the storm is his nature, and as much as I would like him to squash McCain like a bug, it really is not the change he has called for. Despite my own postdebate despair, in many analyses Obama was judged the winner.

We watched the vice-presidential debate in the privacy of our own home. While Rove and Limbaugh, the Diaxis of Evil, had their old crank-yanker with the dicey health records hooked up to adrenalized life support, they had their VP candidate hooked up to the info-injection machine. They want her ready when they pull McCain's plug. She is a quick study. After a few sessions of cramming, when

Katie Couric pulled her neck string, Palin answered, "Putin rears his head, flies over, in the airspace, where does he go, Alaska." There were some info-sequencing glitches, but their Manchurian Candidate was deemed Being There brilliant. Just as eight years ago when the bar was set low for Bush, if Sarah Palin did not burst into flames, she would be proclaimed the winner.

It is not the parroting of insta-info that gets me. It is the affect of the wink.

I come from a family of winkers. I swear if my family had been on the *Titanic,* the last thing I would have seen my dad do as he sank beneath the cold dark waves would have been one last wink and gone.

Our wink could be quick and crisp, a nano-flick that moved few other facial muscles. It could be slow and tight, a cyclopean clench that suggested Bell's palsy. It was intentional or automatic. It was a family facial semaphore with several meanings: "Good morning." "He doesn't know what he's talking about." "I'm just joshing you." "We're in this together." It was by turns welcoming, mocking, denying, reassuring, and conspiratorial.

Like many family tics, we never noticed it, until a friend visited for the weekend and asked afterward, "Why do you all wink at each other?" "We do?" "Are you kidding? All the time. Walking into a room. When someone else is talking. At first I thought your brother was flirting with me at dinner. He just wanted the mashed potatoes."

Thanks to my long experience decoding winks, I just caught the very tail end of Sarah Palin's VP debate wink as one perfectly made-up eyelid rose again to the open position. "Did she just wink?" I asked. I had been momentarily distracted, not by daubing my Palin bingo card (I did not win) but by turning to shush my grousing gal pal. "Haven't you got cleaning to do?" As I turned back, I saw the vapor trail of what I knew was a wink. Damn!

Moderator Gwen Ifill had been drudged all week as partisan because she is writing a book about the new generation of black politicians. That was no reason for them to break her ankle. Ifill did her level best, though she did not ask one question about immigration or abortion. Could Palin have pulled another answer out of her energy package? Palin, the inexperienced Reaganette, attempted to "there-

you-go-again" Biden's experience and establish rapport not with the politicos out there on the East Coast but with the mind-if-I-call-you-Joe-Six-Packs in Smallville, U.S.A.

Like Biden, I also got choked up during the debate. Sadly, the only moment of unanimity of the night was that both candidates oppose gay marriage. Biden, who has perfected the art of not answering questions with many, many words, chose the moment to say tersely, "I am against gay marriage." Apparently the B of LGBT stands for bipartisan, not bisexual. Palin practically rubbed her hands in glee and chirped tolerantly, "I'm so glad we agree on that, Joe." After all our LGBT support and hard work for the Obama-Biden ticket, it was sickening. Mind if I call you chicken, Joe?

After a few post-Palin-selection performances, audience members came up to me and told me that I had gone too easy on her. They wanted blood. After all the justifiable complaining I had done about the sexism in Hillary Clinton's primary bid, it was true, I had a hard time being hard on Sarah Palin. Even with her inflammatory insouciance, she is so beside the point.

She is Operation Distraction from John McCain, careening around answering a question about Spain with all the loopiness of Miss Teen South Carolina when asked why one-fifth of Americans cannot locate the United States on a map. Such as.

What I find staggering is that in the midst of wars and financial collapse, we are talking seriously and at all about McCain's Folly. Sarah Palin is a folksy, well-trained, Wikipedia-deep, by-George-she's-got-it bush to nowhere. Fine for governor up there in Alaska but not for vice president down here on Planet Earth. She is in way over her head. She will wink just before we all sink.

I predict a Palin Effect. People will tell pollsters that they are supporting Palin, go into the voting booth, flash on their vanished 401(k)s, and vote otherwise.

......................................................................................

# The Right to Comfort

## October 2008

My actual brother Bill Clinton was an early, enthusiastic supporter of Barack Obama. My sister-in-law Mary was, like me, a Hilary supporter. Their forty-year marriage easily withstood all the good-natured back-and-forth at the dinner table. They both are active, feet-on-the-street, door-knocking Dems in a heavily Republican enclave. After Obama won the Democratic primary, they hosted several potluck brunches in their home near Philadelphia to heal the rift between Clinton and Obama supporters. They want to win the White House in November.

My brother is an optimist of epic proportions. He loves to "engage" with anyone over national, state, city, and local politics. He ran as a Democrat and won a spot on his local entrenched-Republican city council. He takes his civic responsibility very seriously and somehow joyously. I am very proud of him.

As he often does, he called me while crawling in traffic on his way to his business school teaching job in central Philly. We chatted about the campaigns, the conventions. He was grimly insulted by the cynicism of McCain's choice of the inexperienced Palin. For once I was the one talking him out of a political funk. What had finally sent him into a slough of despond was the remark of a fellow worker: "Bill, I just can't vote for a black man."

And whup, there it was. We both tried to see the upside in such a bald statement. At least he was clear. No so-called Bradley effect there. In 1982, when the African-American mayor of L.A., Tom Bradley, ran for governor of California, he was ahead in the polls. When voters cast their ballots in the privacy of their own booths, they did not vote for Bradley. My brother and I tried to put a positive spin on his coworker's statement. It was somehow progress that he was so open about his racism.

Given where my brother and I came from, it was progress that we

were even having the conversation. Our parents were raised in South Buffalo. I can recall my uncles and aunts venting about "the Negroes." Trust me, there was more. We were raised in upstate New York, in all-white schools and neighborhoods. Though my dad never said anything as overt as what he had heard when he was growing up, he was appalled when I drove him through the neighborhood where I rented my first apartment. He said he worried about my safety. My mother began nattering at me to make sure I locked my doors.

The civil rights movement of the 1960s and the assassination of Martin Luther King jolted us out of our segregated ignorance. Those old uncles and aunts have died. My mom and dad are gone. Hard-won integration in both school and work and a growing black middle class have helped all of my siblings form activist relationships and some black friendships my parents could never have imagined. Clearly I mistook my own personal progress for some kind of national progress, despite the ominous conversations with my younger sister, whose two kids went to a predominantly black public high school and could not wait to get out.

My brother Bill also loves a good push-back, so he asked his coworker why he could not vote for a black man. Joe, the coworker, said that he had worked with black people and they just were not qualified for their jobs. Again the push: Bill asked if he had never worked with unqualified white people.

As he drove, speaking into his window visor, Bill recreated the strained conversation, and we talked some more about the racism of the race. The inevitable cracks about a black man in the White House. The stories of Obama hanged in effigy by four high school students. The faux questions: Is Obama black enough? Is this the end of black politics? These bogus questions were asked while the real questions about disproportionate numbers of blacks caught in subprime scams, the HIV crisis among black women, incarceration rates among young black men were not asked.

Bill pulled into his parking lot as I was telling him about a friend who told me his father said he was going to vote for Obama but seemed to imply simultaneously his dismay that there was not someone better out there to vote for.

As if it has been a picnic doing jokes about the recent white presi-

dent, I am frequently asked if it will be difficult to do jokes about a black president. The assumption is of course that I will do material about blackness. But that is not my area of expertise. Whiteness is. And where I come from and where I often perform, questioning whiteness is like fish questioning water. Fish do not question water until it is not there. And it is a very short Q&A, unless the lucky fish is tossed back into the water. Recently exposed to air, the fish asks, "Was that the water thing you were talking about?"

Once in India with my girlfriend, I was the only white person in a sea of brown people. I was stunned to find how I navigated the discomfort of my difference by reassuring myself of my white superiority. By luck of birth, I was born into the right white skin. I'm number one. I deserve my job, my home, my good health, because I am white. I told her what I was thinking. We were both distressed, and race remains an ongoing conversation in our relationship.

Questioning my own assumption of white superiority—for that is the water I swim in—is the challenge represented by a black president. It is not his job. It is mine. I feel lucky and excited, though like a fish gasping in air, it will not be comfortable. Like many white Americans, I fear discomfort. But tell me, where in the Bill of Rights is the right to comfort? The good news is that I already have the aqualung and swim fins I purchased for swimming upstream against sexism and homophobia.

.................................................................................

# The Big Gay Slowdown
## November 2008

One cool evening in Provincetown, I was raccoon-proofing a trash can at the end of the driveway. A big pickup truck with muted purple running lights glided up. The tinted window slid down and the driver, a young, spike-haired, neighbor dyke, stuck her elbow out the win-

dow, leaned out slightly, and said helpfully, "Better tell the wife to get the cats in."

"Excuse me?"

She repeated gruffly, "Y' better tell the wife to get the cats in. Coyotes." She pulled away as I gave a confused, halfhearted thanks.

In our house, we have epi-pens for allergic reactions to cats, not cats. I like birds too much. One cat-loving friend accused me of keeping a coyote to keep the local cat population down. And I do not have a wife.

Despite much good-natured pressure, my partner of twenty years and I have not gotten married. If we ever do marry, I know I will want an old-fashioned wedding. Really old-fashioned. When I get married, I want a country. Not a wife.

The word *wife* induces involuntary shuddering in me. From an early age I was against marriage. I never got the marriage/bridal gene. When my little girlfriends role-played weddings, I thought they were dorks. Especially if I did not get to play the groom.

I have always thought marriage was a means of social control designed for the profligation of the species. My early inchoate notion was supported by my later feminism: woman is property; property is theft. I like to think that if I were straight I would not have gotten married, despite the velvet-hammered pressure of my Irish-Catholic mother.

For me, becoming a lesbian had two big attractions: I would not have to get married or have children. Of course, the biggest attraction was the one I had my sophomore year in college for a hot, smart, sarcastic woman named Ann. She kissed like a hungry angel.

Truth be told—and it so rarely is—I probably do not like gay marriage as much as any anti-gay so-called Christian nutbucket. I am the Mr. Big of gay marriage. Luckily, my partner feels the same way. And yet I completely support the freedom to marry for all gay people. I believe my friends when they tell me how surprised they are at the transformational power of declaring their love before family and friends. I love hearing their stories.

I hate hearing their stories of the on-the-ground, hand-to-hand combat against antigay ballot initiatives in Florida, Arizona (again), and California. In California, two newly wedded lesbian friends called

mé as they drove to yet another "No on 8" rally through a thicket of "Yes on 8" yard signs. The friend who was driving was distraught because her usually serene partner was having a homicidal screaming jag triggered by all the "Yes" signage. She asked me to talk her down. I suggested she drive on the lawns and take out some signs.

In this financial climate, in California alone, $60 million is being spent for and against the basic human rights of gay people. You would think the attitude would be, "Oh for heaven's sake, it's almost the end of the world—let the gay people get married."

If we defeat Prop Hate, I say we sue our adversaries for antigay harassment and recoup our money. We can use the money to continue to provide for homeless LGBT youth, HIV/AIDS support, and care for our elder gays.

If we do not defeat Prop Hate, I say November 5 we call for a general gay work slowdown.

Decorators will do deliberately bad, possibly dangerous feng shui.

Hairdressers will mistakenly lay hot curling irons down on ears.

Social workers will give bad advice: "Your father sounds like a great guy. Show him some love."

Salespeople will ooze: "Oh, that looks great on you."

Waiters will serve cold food and suggest the wrong wine.

Flight attendants will put OUT OF SERVICE signs on bathrooms midway through long-distance flights.

Some nameless malaise will dim Broadway.

If gay people are not to be full citizens of this country, we should stop paying taxes.

To make up for the lost funds, as an alternate revenue stream, it is time to tax churches that have encouraged antigay hatred through their bullying pulpits. The FBI recently released hate-crime statistics that showed a 1 percent decrease in hate crimes overall but a 6 percent increase in antigay hate crimes.

When and if I get married, I want my country. Call me old-fashioned.

# Afterword

I write this afterword the week after the election of Barack Obama as president of the United States of America. Michelle Obama is the first lady. A week later and those two incredible facts are still true! Our long mental curfew is about to be lifted. The Bush S&L scandal of shredding and looting continues as W. promises a vaguely scatological "smooth transition." George has enough accumulated sick days. We are more eager than he for him to take his leave. In fact, there is nothing we would rather give him.

The default prompt of my post-Bush traumatic stress syndrome (PBTSD) is to expect that after this great electoral news, something horrible will surely happen. My habit of dread is enabled by self-justifying holograms of the MSM suddenly adrift without their adrenalized twenty-month campaign story.

So for a while I have turned it off. I have turned to my neighbors, family, and friends instead. In my building's elevator, I see the elegant older black man, a retired city court bailiff. Over the years we have shared our worries about Yankees baseball, Bushworld, the war, and the campaign. We hug and speak of the great victory. He never stops shaking his head in disbelief. I talk to my brother Bill as he drives to work, his voice hoarse from a raucous caucus of victorious Pennsylvania Democrats. At dinners with friends we talk about where we were and how we celebrated on election night.

And we talk about what it means to us. One friend, a loud African-American queen, said, somberly for him, how he worries for Barack's safety and fears that he will not be critical enough of Barack because of how much he loves him. Then, of course, he launched into a deconstruction of Michelle Obama's election night red and black dress.

Like many Americans, my job is in flux. During the Bush regime,

what was bad for us was good for me. A comedy gold mine of hypocrisy, mangled language, and venal caricatures made my task easy. But my own selfish worries about the hard work of suddenly being an insider with the election of a progressive-centrist were premature. With the passage of Prop Hate ballots in California, Florida, Arizona, and Arkansas, my job, with its outsider perspective, is secure for a few more years. Think "Yes on Kate."

At a gathering a few nights after the election, and after the awkward mandatory celebratory white fist bumps, a woman asked my partner and me, "And *what* happened in California?" My gal pal responded, "Straight people were unable to support the moral equality of gay people." The woman pulled her head back, frowned slightly, repeated the words as if they were a new and difficult language, and said, "Hmm—I'll have to remember that."

My job will be to remind her. That the ballot initiatives were not about the moral sanctity of straight marriage being inexplicably undermined by gay marriage. That we experienced the Bradley effect. That straight progressives need to champion the rights of gay people. Especially you whom we worked to elect, President Obama. I am sure I can fashion a bon mot linking Sarah Palin and gay people and being thrown under the Straight Talk Express bus.

My job will also be to remind the LGBT community in our painful post-initiative feedback sessions that religion is the opposite of the people. While black churches were certainly instrumental in passing antigay initiatives, white churches cannot get off Dred Scott free. Multiwived Mormons poured millions into Prop Hate. The U.S. Conference of Catholic Bishops, with its zero experience of marriage, contributed thousands.

My job will be to remind LGBT people that we cannot win if our own people do not care. If we remain partially or fully closeted and do not openly support gay organizations that train those much-maligned but highly effective "community organizers" and leaders, we will never win full equality. We are forty years removed from the Stonewall Riots. We must think, Yes, *we* can.

*Yesvember 2008*

# Acknowledgments

Thanks to Amy Hoffman of the *Women's Review of Books,* Matt Rothschild of the *Progressive,* and Anne Stockwell of the *Advocate* for publishing some of these essays. Thanks to Tam Martin, my artist representative, for booking me on the stages where many of these essays began. Thanks to Michele Karlsberg, my publicist and promoter, for making sure I wrote them. Thanks to K.B. and Champa Vaid for being writers and artists and for your daughter.